Salvation through Jesus Christ:
Basics of Forgiveness under the Gospel

by David E. Pratte

**Available in print at
www.gospelway.com/sales**

Salvation through Jesus Christ:
Basics of Forgiveness under the Gospel

© Copyright David E. Pratte, 2019
All rights reserved

ISBN: 9781097192717
Imprint: Independently published

Note carefully: No teaching in any of our materials is intended or should ever be construed to justify or to in any way incite or encourage personal vengeance or physical violence against any person.

"He who glories, let him glory in the Lord" – 1 Corinthians 1:31

Front page photo

"For these things were done that the Scripture should be fulfilled, ... 'They shall look on Him whom they pierced.'" – John 19:36,67 (NKJV)

Photo Credit: Public domain via Wikimedia Commons

Other Acknowledgements

Unless otherwise indicated, Scripture quotations are generally from the New King James Version (NKJV), copyright 1982, 1988 by Thomas Nelson, Inc. used by permission. All rights reserved.

Scripture quotations marked (NASB) are from *Holy Bible, New American Standard* La Habra, CA: The Lockman Foundation, 1995.

Scripture quotations marked (ESV) are from *The Holy Bible, English Standard Version*, copyright ©2001 by Crossway Bibles, a publishing ministry of Good News Publishers. Used by permission. All rights reserved.

Scripture quotations marked (MLV) are from Modern Literal Version of The New Testament, Copyright 1999 by G. Allen Walker.

Scripture quotations marked (NRSV) are from the New Revised Standard Version of the Bible, copyright 1989 by the Division of Christian Education, National Council of the Churches of Christ in the United States of America.

Scripture quotations marked (NIV) are from the New International Version of the Holy Bible, copyright 1978 by Zondervan Bible publishers, Grand Rapids, Michigan.

Scripture quotations marked (HCSB) are from the Holman Christian Standard Bible, copyright 2008 by Holman Bible publishers, Nashville, Tennessee.

Other Books by the Author

Topical Bible Studies

Why Believe in God, Jesus, and the Bible? (evidences)
True Words of God: Bible Inspiration and Preservation
"It Is Written": The Authority of the Bible
Salvation through Jesus Christ: Basics of Forgiveness
Grace, Faith, and Obedience: The Gospel or Calvinism?
Growing a Godly Marriage & Raising Godly Children
The God of the Bible (study of the Father, Son, and Holy Spirit)
Kingdom of Christ: Future Millennium or Present Spiritual Reign?
Do Not Sin Against the Child: Abortion, Unborn Life, & the Bible

Commentaries on Bible Books

Genesis	*Proverbs*	*Ephesians*
Joshua and Ruth	*Ecclesiastes*	*Philippians &*
Judges	*Gospel of Matthew*	*Colossians*
1 Samuel	*Gospel of Mark*	*1 & 2 Thessalonians*
2 Samuel	*Gospel of John*	*Hebrews*
1 Kings	*Acts*	*James and Jude*
2 Kings	*Romans*	*1 and 2 Peter*
Ezra, Nehemiah, Esther	*Galatians*	*1,2,3 John*
Job		

Bible Question Class Books

Genesis	*Ecclesiastes*	*2 Corinthians and*
Joshua and Ruth	*Isaiah*	*Galatians*
Judges	*Daniel*	*Ephesians and*
1 Samuel	*Hosea, Joel, Amos,*	*Philippians*
2 Samuel	*Obadiah*	*Colossians, 1&2*
1 Kings	*Gospel of Matthew*	*Thessalonians*
2 Kings	*Gospel of Mark*	*1 & 2 Timothy,*
Ezra, Nehemiah,	*Gospel of Luke*	*Titus, Philemon*
Esther	*Gospel of John*	*Hebrews*
Job	*Acts*	*James – Jude*
Proverbs	*Romans*	*Revelation*
	1 Corinthians	

Workbooks with Study Notes

Jesus Is Lord: Workbook on the Fundamentals of the Gospel of Christ
Following Jesus: Workbook on Discipleship
God's Eternal Purpose in Christ: Workbook on the Theme of the Bible
· *Family Reading Booklist*

Visit our website at www.gospelway.com/sales to see a current list of books in print.

Other Resources from the Author

Printed books, booklets, and tracts available at
www.gospelway.com/sales
Free Bible study articles online at
www.gospelway.com
Free Bible courses online at www.biblestudylessons.com
Free class books at www.biblestudylessons.com/classbooks
Free commentaries on Bible books at
www.biblestudylessons.com/commentary
Contact the author at
www.gospelway.com/comments

Abbreviations Used in These Notes

ASV – American Standard Version
b/c/v – book, chapter, and verse
ESV – English Standard Version
f – the following verse
ff – the following verses
HCSB – Holman Christian Standard Bible
KJV – King James Version
MLV – Modern Literal Version
NASB – New American Standard Bible
NEB – New English Bible
NIV – New International Version
NKJV – New King James Version
NRSV – New Revised Standard Version
RSV – Revised Standard Version

Table of Contents

What Sin Has Done for You 7
Jesus: Your Savior 15
Things Essential to Salvation 23
The Importance of Hearing the Gospel 30
What Must We Believe? 38
The Importance of Obedience 46
Godly Sorrow or Worldly Sorrow? 55
Repentance 63
Confession of Christ 71
The Action of Baptism 79
Should Babies Be Baptized? 87
The Purpose of Baptism 99
Should an Alien Sinner Pray for Forgiveness? 107
Are You Really "Born Again"? 114
Will All Devout, Moral People Be Saved? 122
A New Man 129
The Importance of Jesus' Church 137
Let Us Return to the Lord 145
How Many Ways to Salvation through Jesus? 153

(Due to printer reformatting, the above numbers may be off a page or two.)

You may find that major topics of this material will repeat topics or concepts covered elsewhere. This serves to emphasize these points and allows each major topic of study to be complete of itself (so major sections can be studied independently).

Note: Unless otherwise indicated, Bible quotations are from the New King James Version. Often – especially when I do not use quotations marks – I am not quoting any translation but simply paraphrasing the passage in my own words.

What Sin Has Done for You

Introduction:

Things in life are not always as advertised.

Have you ever bought a product only to be really disappointed in it? Karen and I once bought a used freezer. When we first examined it, it felt cold inside. But it was sitting in a garage in the wintertime. The man said it worked; but when we got it home, it did not work at all.

Commercials can make a product sound so good you are supposed to think you can't live without it. But many of the products advertised are not good for you at all. Often the reality is entirely different from what is advertised.

Likewise, sin puts on a good front, but the reality is much different.

Sin is transgression of God's law (1 John 3:4). Pure and simple, sin is disobeying our Creator.

Some people try to convince us that sin is harmless, innocent, and even enjoyable.

Hebrews 11:25 refers to the "pleasures of sin."

James 1:14,15 – Sin entices us by appealing to our desires. We may truly enjoy some aspects of sin temporarily. But despite the apparent advantages, the end result is tragic.

The purpose of this lesson is to examine the real consequences of sin.

Genesis 2:16,17 – God created everything "very good." But He warned the first man and woman about the consequences of sin.

Nevertheless, Eve sinned and encouraged Adam to sin, and since then all people have sinned (Romans 3:23). Tragic consequences have resulted.

In this lesson we want to consider, not just what sin advertises and promises, but what it really delivers: the reality of sin. Consider what sin has done for you and all of the human race.

Consequences of Sin in This Life

People like to convince themselves that sinners live "the good life." They think God makes up rules to take away people's fun, so to really enjoy life you have to ignore the rules. This is what sin advertises, but consider what sin really causes.

Sickness, Pain, and Death

Genesis 3:16,19 – The world was free from suffering and death until Adam and Eve sinned. Their sin brought pain and death into the world. This includes disease, which causes death.

All sickness and death are a result of sin.

1 Corinthians 15:21,22,25,26 – Everyone dies as result of Adam's sin. Death is an enemy, because it is a consequence of sin.

John 11:35 – Jesus wept at death of Lazarus. Death was sad, even to Jesus.

When a person dies, some people say, "It was the will of God." But death is the consequence of sin, and it was never God's will for man to sin. Death is God's will only in the same sense that it is the will of a parent to punish a disobedient child. Neither the parent nor the child is glad the punishment must occur. But when a child does wrong, the parent must correct him.

We may or may not be able to see a direct connection between sin and sickness.

Sometimes we see the connection between sin and suffering.

* A man gets drunk and has a wreck.

* Smoking leads to cancer, drinking to cirrhosis, fornication to V.D.

* Anytime there is war, someone has been guilty of greed, anger, hatred, or a lust for power. There would be no war if everyone would live right.

Salvation through Jesus Christ

Other times we may not see how a specific sin led to a specific disease or death.

But whenever a loved one suffers or dies, remember this is what sin has done for mankind.

2 Corinthians 12:7-10 – Paul prayed for God to remove his thorn in the flesh. It is right to pray for God to help us overcome sickness and suffering, but God chose to leave the problem for Paul's good. God has not promised to remove all suffering from our lives on earth. Suffering reminds us that sin is tragic.

1 Corinthians 15:21-16 – In the end Christ will remove all death by raising the dead.

Obstacles and Frustration

Genesis 3:17-19 – As a consequence of sin, man would face problems, hindrances, and difficulties in his work. Life is filled with thorns and thistles. People face many hardships in achieving goals.

Problems in daily work

Men work long hours and face conflicts on the job. Other workers may fail to do their job, supervisors may make poor decisions, equipment may fail, and the government requires red tape. Every man I know can talk for hours about the frustrations on his job.

Homemakers may think their work never gets caught up. As you do the laundry, the kids start to fight, the baby needs changed, a salesman knocks at the door, and the dinner burns.

Problems in the church

We may think there should be no problems in the work of the church, but God's word shows otherwise. We often struggle to find people who are willing to study God's word. When we do find someone, some false teacher leads him astray. Some members become inactive or fall away, or members fuss among themselves. And there always seems to be some new doctrinal issue.

When these problems occur, we should remember that this is what sin has done for mankind. Why should we believe people who tell us that sin is better than God's way?

Alienation Between People

Advertisements for bars and casinos show people having a wonderful social life. But how does sin really affect human relationships?

Alienation within families

Brothers and sisters

Genesis 4:3-8 – Sin alienated Adam and Eve's sons. In the end, Cain became angry and killed Abel.

Genesis 27 – Jacob had to leave home because his deceit caused Esau to threaten to kill him.

Genesis 37 – Joseph's brothers sold him as a slave because they were jealous.

Likewise, children today often fight and quarrel.

Husbands and wives

Many homes are often divided or end in divorce because of disobedience to God's word.

Ephesians 5:22-25,28 – God teaches husbands to love their wives and wives to submit to their husbands. But sometimes husbands are selfish or wives rebel.

The happiness of a home may be destroyed by alcohol or drugs, gambling, adultery, etc.

God's way is best, but again and again we hear of homes broken because of sin.

Parents and children

Luke 15:11-32 – The prodigal son rejected his father's will and wasted his inheritance in immorality.

2 Samuel 15-18 – David fought a war with his own son Absalom.

Ephesians 6:1-4 – God says children should obey parents, and parents should discipline children in love for their good. But we often hear of parents becoming physically violent or even abandoning a child. Or children may rebel, reject God, or turn to drinking and drugs, sexual immorality, or crime.

How can anyone say that sin is better than God's way?

Alienation between friends or between church members

People may be close friends for years but become alienated when one mistreats or takes advantage of the other.

2 Timothy 4:10 – Because he loved this world, Demas forsook Paul. Brethren who worked side-by-side for years, may be so alienated and bitter that they cannot even worship together.

Romans 12:18 – God teaches us how to avoid and resolve our differences. But this requires all parties to cooperate. Sometimes, no matter how we try, others refuse to be peaceable.

This is what sin has done for mankind! Why should anyone think sin is a better way to live than serving God?

Alienation from God

Adam and Eve were alienated from God because of sin.

Genesis 3:8 – They had been in God's presence, but sin caused them to hide from God.

Genesis 2:16,17 – The "death" man received because of sin refers primarily to spiritual death: separation from God. Physical death is separation of body from spirit (James 2:26). Spiritual death is separation of man from God.

We too are alienated from God because of our sins.

Isaiah 59:1,2 – Our sins and iniquities separate us from God.

Ephesians 2:1-3,12 – Sin makes us spiritually dead while physically alive. We are separated from Christ, without hope and without God.

Colossians 1:21-23 – In sin, we are enemies of God. The blessing of the gospel is that, through Christ, we can be forgiven of sin and be reconciled with God. Physical problems may or may not be removed in this life, but the problem of alienation from God can be completely solved through Christ.

God created man in His image (Genesis 1:26,27), so we could have fellowship and peace with God. Instead, sin so alienates us that He considers us His enemy. But by following God's way, we can be friends of God again. So how can sin be better for man than God's way?

(Ephesians 4:18; 5:6; Romans 5:10; 1:18; 2:5; James 4:4; Colossians 3:6)

Mental Anguish

People in sin are often pictured as carefree, just enjoying life to the full. But consider what problems the Bible says sinners have:

Guilt

Genesis 3:10 – Adam **hid** from God because he knew he was naked.

Psalm 38:3-8 – David's guilt caused pain, sorrow, and inward groaning. (51:1-3)

Matthew 27:3-5 – Judas killed himself because of his guilt.

Jonah 1,2 – Jonah tried to run and hide from God, but no one can hide from God.

God is willing to forgive us and remove the burden of guilt. Yet many people live in anguish year after year, **knowing** they are guilty. This is what sin has done for mankind.

Fear, insecurity, and worry

Matthew 6:25-34 – Many people worry about how they will obtain what they want in life. But God promises to care for His servants.

Philippians 4:6,7 – Many people are anxious about life because they don't serve God or don't pray to Him in faith. But God promises peace that passes understanding if His faithful servants pray in faith.

Matthew 25:46 – Many fear death because they aren't ready for judgment. But God promises eternal life to the righteous.

So these consequences of sin can definitely be solved by the power of God even in this life. So why continue to suffer in sin? How much better to serve God and let Him remove the burden of guilt!

Sorrow

Matthew 26:75 – Peter wept bitterly after he had denied Christ three times.

Psalm 32:1-5 – David groaned all day long because of sin, but when he confessed he was forgiven. Once again, the burden of guilt on our souls can be completely lifted through Jesus.

So why would anyone think that sin is better than God's way? Does it make sense to continue in sin instead of serving God?

(Psalm 38:3-8; Proverbs 13:15)

Consequences of Sin after This Life

So far we have described problems sin causes **in this life**. But some people seem to suffer little if any consequences of sin in this life. They may prosper and appear to live "the high life." So some folks conclude that maybe sin is not all that bad.

The truth is that most people in sin do suffer many of the problems we have described in this life, whether they acknowledge it or not. But after this life will come problems that everyone will definitely suffer unless their sins are forgiven.

Sinners Receive Eternal Punishment.

Consider how the Bible describes this punishment.

Fire

Matthew 25:41 – The wicked will go to eternal fire prepared for the Devil and his angels.

Revelation 20:10-15 – The second death is a lake of fire for all not found in book of life.

Physical death is the first death, and we have learned it is the consequence of sin. But that death is nothing compared to the **second** death: the lake of fire.

(Matthew 13:39-42; 18:8,9)

Conscious torment

Revelation 20:10 – Those in the lake of fire were tormented day and night.

Luke 16:19-31 – The rich man died and was **tormented** in flame.

(Romans 2:8,9)

Outer darkness

Matthew 8:12 – Imagine being tormented in flame, but you can't see anything. You want to escape, but there is no way to escape.

There is not one passage that says anything good about the state of the wicked after death.

Eternal

Matthew 25:41,46 – Eternal fire, everlasting punishment

2 Thessalonians 1:8,9 – Everlasting destruction (ruin)

This is the final result of what sin does for mankind. We will see that the gospel shows how to avoid this end. But why would anyone defend sin or present it as harmless and innocent?

Sinners Miss Eternal Life

Not only does sin lead to a horrible destiny, but it also causes us to miss a beautiful destiny. Notice how the gospel describes the destiny of those who are forgiven of sin.

Heaven, the dwelling place of God

Matthew 5:10-12 – Those who endure persecution receive a great reward in **heaven**.

1 Peter 1:3,4 – An inheritance incorruptible, undefiled, reserved in Heaven.

1 Thessalonians 4:17; 5:9,10 – We shall ever be with the Lord living with Him.

(Philippians 3:20,21; Revelation 21:3; 22:3,4)

Happiness with no suffering

Romans 2:6-10 – Glory, honor, and peace to all who work good

Revelation 21:3,4 – God will wipe away all tears, death, sorrow, crying, and pain.

When God first created man, everything was "very good" with no problems. But sin brought with it all the problems we have discussed. So now God has provided another place where these problems are not found. Why would anyone prefer the consequences of sin?

Eternal life

Matthew 25:46 – The righteous go into eternal life.

Romans 6:23 – The gift of God is eternal life through Jesus Christ.

Revelation 21:27 – Those who practice sin will not enter Heaven (verse 8).

Sin not only makes this life miserable and causes physical death, but after death it causes us to miss the joys of heaven. This is what sin has done for mankind.

(Romans 2:7; Galatians 6:8; Titus 1:2; 3:7; John 3:16; 20:31)

Conclusion

Knowing the truth of God's word, why should anyone want to defend sin as being innocent or harmless, let alone pleasant and desirable? Why would anyone continue practicing sin?

The good news of the gospel is that Jesus Christ can solve all these problems.

The gospel means "good news." God seeks our good, not our harm. But no one will truly appreciate the good news till he first understands the bad news.

John 3:16 – Jesus can forgive sin so we can have eternal life, not eternal torment. (1 John 1:6,7; Romans 5:1,2)

Philippians 4:13 – I can do all things through Christ who strengthens me. He gives His people strength to endure and be faithful despite the hardships of life.

Serving God does not remove all problems from the lives of Christians. All people suffer in this life because sin is in the world. But God helps us avoid many of the problems in this life. Then after this life, we can go to a land where there are no problems at all.

What must we do to be forgiven and receive eternal life?

Believe, repent, confess, and be baptized – Mark 16:16; Acts 2:38.

Live a faithful life – Revelation 2:10; 1 Corinthians 15:58.

If we sin again, repent and confess – 1 John 1:8-10; Acts 8:22.

Have you been forgiven, so you can escape the consequences of sin? Are you living a faithful life so you have assurance of eternal life with no problems when this life is over?

Jesus: Your Savior

Introduction:

When I was eight years old, I almost drowned.

Some neighbor kids and I made wooden boats and floated them in a drainage ditch near our house. A neighbor warned us the ditch was deep and the water was muddy; we could drown if we fell in. My boat floated under a bridge and, as I reached out from the shore to grab it, I slowly slid into the water.

I couldn't swim. I remember going under twice and was on the way down for the third time. Meanwhile the kids were up on the bridge screaming. The neighbor who had warned us was getting ready to go to town; a few minutes later and he would not have been home. But he heard the noise and jumped in to pull me out. He could not see me in the muddy water; but as he jumped in, he kicked me and pulled me out.

I remember saying, "You saved my life. You saved my life."

Most people understand the concept of a person who saves someone else.

We sometimes hear in the news of people who risk their lives to save someone else: firemen, policemen, etc.

The Bible often refers to God, especially Jesus, as our Savior.

John 4:42 — The Samaritans said, "...we have heard for ourselves and know that this is indeed the Christ, the Savior of the world."

"Savior" means one who saves, delivers, or rescues others from peril, danger, or calamity.

The purpose of this study is to consider the Bible teaching about Jesus as Savior.

We want to consider some examples in which God has saved people from various dangers throughout history. We will consider specifically what it means to you and me today: why do we need Jesus as our Savior? Then we will consider what Jesus did so we could be saved, and what we must do to receive His salvation.

Consider the following facts about Jesus as our Savior:

Examples of Divine Salvation

The Bible reveals a pattern that God has repeatedly saved people from danger and destruction. Consider some Old Testament examples:

* **Lot** – Genesis 19:19 – God destroyed Sodom and Gomorrah for their evil, but He first sent Lot out. Lot said (to the angel) that he had shown mercy and had saved Lot's life. Note that God punishes the wicked, but saves the righteous.

* **Jacob and his family** – Genesis 50:20 (45:7) – Joseph's brothers had sold him as a slave into Egypt. Eventually he became governor of the land and brought his family there to keep them alive through a famine. He said that his brothers had meant to do him harm, but God used it to save many people alive. Note that God used the evil of wicked people to bring salvation to the righteous.

* **Israel at the Red Sea** – Exodus 14:13 (15:2) – When Israel was trapped between the Egyptian army and the Red Sea, Moses said to not be afraid but see the salvation of the Lord. God opened the sea so they passed on dry ground, then caused it to collapse and kill the Egyptians. Note that the means God used to save the righteous also became a means to punish the wicked.

* **Gideon and Israel** – Judges 7:2,7 – God deliberately reduced the size of Gideon's army so they would not think they had saved themselves by their own hand. Instead, God said He would save them from the Midianites. Note that God requires men to act in order for Him to save them, but He makes clear that He Himself is the one who saved them. (6:14,15,36,37)

* **David and Israel** – 1 Samuel 17:47 – When David faced Goliath, he said that God does not save by sword or spear, but He would give victory over Goliath.

These and other examples illustrate the concept of a savior. A savior rescues or delivers others from peril or hardship. The examples show that God can deliver people from problems that no one else can solve. When our situation seems hopeless and helpless, when we are powerless to save ourselves, that is when we need a Savior. God is the ultimate Savior. Only He has the solution to our greatest needs.

(Matthew 14:30; 2 Chronicles 32:22; Jeremiah 42:11; Nehemiah 9:27; Daniel 6:27; Numbers 10:9; 1 Samuel 7:8; 14:23; 2 Kings 19:34; 2 Chronicles 20:9; Hebrews 11:7; 2 Peter 2:5)

Your Need and My Need for a Savior

Old Testament examples show that God has power to rescue people from danger or calamity from which they are powerless to save themselves. But why do you and I need a savior? What great danger or calamity do we face?

Jesus Saves from Sin

Matthew 1:21 — Before Jesus was born, the angel promised Joseph that Mary would bring forth a Son. He said to "call His name Jesus, for He will save His people from their sins." "Jesus" means "Jehovah is salvation" (or Jehovah is the Savior). But the salvation Jesus would bring was salvation from **sin**. (Luke 2:11)

Luke 19:10 – Jesus came to seek and to save that which was **lost**. The reason man needs salvation is that he is lost in sin and cannot solve the problem by himself.

Acts 5:31 – God exalted Jesus to His right hand to be a prince and Savior and to give **repentance and forgiveness of sins**. So the reason we need salvation is that we are guilty of sin. To be saved we need to repent so Jesus can forgive our sins.

1 Timothy 1:15 — This is a faithful saying and worthy of all acceptance, that Christ Jesus came into the world to save sinners. Sin is transgression of God's law (1 John 3:4). The consequences of sin are such that sinners are condemned to eternal punishment and cannot save themselves.

1 Thessalonians 5:8,9 — God did not appoint us to wrath, but to obtain salvation through our Lord Jesus Christ. Our sins make us God's enemies, doomed to suffer eternal wrath. This wrath is described as a second death in a lake of fire (Rev. 20). But this is not what God wants for us. He wants us to be saved from sin through His Son.

This is the salvation that God offers through Jesus under the gospel.

(Romans 5:9,10; James 5:19,20; 2 Timothy 1:10; Hebrews 2:2,3; Titus 2:13,14; Romans 6:23; Luke 1:77)

Salvation from Sin Is a Universal Need.

Many people do not appreciate the salvation Jesus offers because they do not realize they need it. But all people become sinners, so everyone needs salvation.

Jesus offers salvation to all people.

John 4:42 – The Samaritans said they had learned that Jesus is the Savior of the **world**.

Titus 2:11 – The grace of God that brings salvation has appeared to **all** men.

1 Timothy 2:3,4,6 – God our Savior desires **all** men to be saved and come to the knowledge of the truth. This is why Christ gave Himself as a ransom for **all.**

Romans 1:16 – The gospel is the power of God to salvation to **everyone** who believes, Jew and Gentile.

Mark 16:15,16 – This is why the gospel must be preached to every creature in the whole world.

Jesus is not the Savior of just a certain nation or race of people, nor of a certain group predetermined unconditionally before the world began. He offers salvation to everyone in the world, because everyone needs it.

All people eventually commit sin (Romans 3:23). This includes you and me. Our sins alienate us from God and doom us to eternal punishment. Since we have sinned against God, only God can declare the basis on which the sins will be forgiven. We are powerless by ourselves to remove the consequences of sin.

This means you and I need Jesus as our Savior. Only Jesus has the power to save everyone in the whole world from sin. He offers that salvation to all. It is up to you and me to decide whether or not we are willing to meet the conditions to receive it.

(John 12:47; Acts 13:47; 1 John 4:14)

Jesus offers complete salvation from all sins.

Hebrews 7:25 – Jesus is able to save to the uttermost those who come to God through Him. Sometimes people fear that they have committed some sin that can never be forgiven. This is true only of sins for which we will not repent. But if we are willing to completely turn from sin and come to Jesus for forgiveness according to the gospel, He is able to save to the uttermost.

And sometimes people have followed the gospel teaching to be forgiven, yet their consciences still bother them. They fear they are still going to be punished despite the forgiveness. True, there are sometimes consequences of our sins that carry over in this life. And we will always regret the fact we committed sin. But once the sin is forgiven, we are saved to the uttermost. There is simply no more guilt before God.

You and I need salvation by Jesus. No other power in the world can save from sin. Without Him, we are powerless. But His power can save **all** people from the eternal consequences of **all** our sins. Are you willing to accept His salvation?

Jesus' Role in Our Salvation

What did Jesus have to do in order to become our Savior?

Jesus Had to Leave Heaven and Come to Live on Earth as a Man

Luke 19:10 — The Son of Man has **come** to seek and to save that which was lost.

1 Timothy 1:15 — Christ Jesus ***came into the world*** to save sinners.

Before He came to earth, Jesus was in heaven with God the Father, enjoying all the glory and power of Deity. He was the eternal Creator (John 1:1-3). But we His creatures were disobedient and doomed to punishment. God loved us so much He determined a way to avoid this for all who are willing to accept salvation.

Our goal is to leave earth and go to heaven. In order to become our Savior, Jesus had to leave the joys and privileges of heaven to come to earth to live as a man.

(John 3:17)

Jesus Had to Die for Our Sins.

Romans 5:6-10 — When we were without strength – helpless and unable to save ourselves – Christ died for the ungodly. This is how we can be saved from wrath and reconciled to God. This is why Jesus had to come to earth as a man. As God, He could not die. But by becoming a man, he could suffer death and pay the penalty for our sins.

So you and I could be saved from the consequences of sin, Jesus was treated as a sinner. He suffered punishment He did not deserve so we could escape the punishment we do deserve. He suffered and died on the cross. Some people would suffer for a righteous man and maybe for a good man. But Jesus did this for us who are sinners.

Hebrews 9:28 — So Jesus was offered once to bear the sins of many. Our salvation will be complete when He comes again to take us to our eternal reward.

Jesus Had to Rise from the Dead.

Romans 5:10 said we are reconciled by His death and saved by His life. This refers to His life ***after*** His death – i.e., His resurrection from the dead.

Hebrews 2:14 – Through death, He destroyed the power of death. But this required Him to be raised from the dead, thereby proving that someday we will all be raised from the dead (1 Corinthians 15:20-26).

1 Corinthians 15:17 – If Christ did not rise, then our faith is vain and we are still in our sins. Had Jesus not been raised from the dead, Satan would have been the victor. By rising, Jesus proved His superior power over Satan, demonstrating His power to save us from sin.

1 Thessalonians 1:10 – Jesus, whom God raised from the dead, is the One who can deliver us from the wrath to come.

Jesus paid the greatest price anyone could pay to be our Savior. Through His suffering and victory, you and I have the hope of eternal life. What will we do with the opportunity? Do we appreciate how much we need Jesus as our Savior?

(1 Timothy 1:15; 1 John 4:14; Ephesians 5:23,25; 1 Peter 2:24; Hebrews 7:25)

The Application to Us: Conditions We Must Meet to Be Saved

Old Testament Examples Show that God's Salvation Is Conditional.

Some people deny that we need to do anything to be saved. They tell us that Jesus is the Savior, so if we think that we must do something, we are denying or belittling Jesus as Savior. However, every example of salvation that we have studied demonstrates that God offers salvation, but people must act in order to receive it.

* ***Lot*** – Genesis 19:19 – God saved Lot from the destruction of Sodom and Gomorrah, but Lot had to leave the city. Action was required.

* ***Jacob and his family*** – Genesis 50:20 (45:7) – God used Joseph to save his family from the famine. But the people had to travel to Egypt to be saved. Action was required.

* ***Israel at the Red Sea*** – Exodus 14:13 (15:2) – God saved Israel from the Egyptian army by parting the Red Sea. But the people had to march through the sea. Action was required.

* ***Gideon and Israel*** – Judges 7:2,7 – God said He would save Israel by delivering them from the Midianites. But Gideon's men had to surround the enemy camp, blow trumpets, and hold torches. Action was required. (6:14,15,36,37)

* ***David and Israel*** – 1 Samuel 17:47 – God saved David from Goliath, but David still had to fight.

In every case, God was the Savior who met the people's need that they could not meet for themselves. But in every case the people had to act. They had to obey God's command to receive His salvation.

We Must Meet the Conditions of the Gospel so We Can Be Forgiven.

Hebrews 5:9 – Jesus is author of eternal salvation to all who **obey** Him.

Philippians 2:12 – Work out your own salvation with fear and trembling.

We have learned that God offers salvation through Christ to all of us, and we all need that salvation. But just as in Old Testament examples, so today there are requirements we must meet to receive the salvation. As long as we deny or neglect the need for obedience, we will never be saved. (James 2:14-26)

What are the conditions we must meet?

Hear the gospel message

Acts 11:14 – The angel told Cornelius to send for Peter who would tell him words by which he and his house could be **saved**. That message is the gospel.

James 1:21 – James instructs men to receive with meekness the implanted word, which is able to **save** our souls.

(1 Corinthians 1:18,21; 15:2; 2 Timothy 3:15; 2 Peter 2:20)

Believe the gospel

Romans 1:16 – The gospel is the power of God to **salvation** to everyone who believes, Jew and Gentile.

Mark 16:15-16 – Jesus said, "Go into all the world and preach the gospel to every creature. He who believes and is baptized will be **saved**; but he who does not believe will be condemned."

The gospel is the message by which God reveals how we can be saved from sin. To receive that salvation, we must learn and believe the message.

(Romans 10:9,10; Acts 16:31; Ephesians 2:8,9)

Repent of sins

Acts 5:31 – God exalted Jesus to His right hand to be a prince and Savior and give repentance and forgiveness of sins.

2 Corinthians 7:10 — Godly sorrow produces repentance to **salvation**, not to be regretted; but the sorrow of the world produces death.

Repentance requires us to be willing to change our lives to serve God according to the gospel message. When we realize what God has done through Jesus to offer salvation, and when we understand the consequences of not being saved, what sensible person would refuse to repent?

Confess Jesus

Romans 10:9,10 – With the heart one believes to righteousness and with the mouth confession is made to **salvation**.

One must have strong enough conviction about Jesus as his Savior that he is willing to openly profess that he knows who Jesus is and is willing to submit to Him.

Be baptized

Mark 16:15,16 – We have seen that the faith that a person needs in order to be saved is a faith that must lead him to obey Jesus' teaching. Jesus specifically stated that faith must lead to baptism if one is to be **saved**.

1 Peter 3:21 – Baptism also now **saves** us.

Baptism is a condition necessary to receive salvation by the blood of Jesus, because one is baptized into Christ and into His death (Romans 6:3). In baptism, one's sins are washed away (Acts 22:16), so he receives the remission of sins (Acts 2:38).

Live a faithful life

Matthew 10:22 — He who endures to the end will be **saved**.

When people truly understand their need for salvation and the great sacrifice that Jesus made to make salvation possible, surely they should willingly meet the conditions of salvation.

(Acts 2:47; Ephesians 5:23,25; 1:13; 2 Thessalonians 2:10,13; Hebrews 10:39; 1 Corinthians 1:21; 15:2ff; 1 Timothy 4:16; Titus 3:5; Mark 8:35; Luke 9:24; 8:11,12)

Conclusion

God has repeatedly admonished people that He offers salvation that no one else can offer.

Isaiah 43:11 – Besides Me there is no Savior. (45:21,22; Hosea 13:4)

Acts 4:12 — Nor is there salvation in any other, for there is no other name under heaven given among men by which we must be saved.

You and I need salvation that only God can offer. He has proved repeatedly in the past that He does have the power to save. He has sent His only begotten Son to die for our salvation. Will you accept the salvation only He can give?

2 Corinthians 6:2 – Behold, now is the accepted time; behold, now is the day of salvation. Why not receive the salvation God offers today?

Let us consider in more detail many of the truths we have introduced so far in this study.

Things Essential to Salvation

Introduction:
Among people who respect the Bible, one point of general agreement is that all people become guilty of sin.
1 John 3:4 — Sin is transgression of (disobedience to) God's law.
Romans 3:23 — Everyone has committed sin. (1 John 1:8,10)
Unfortunately, those who profess to believe the Bible do not always agree about what God requires us to do about our sins.
Often people find something that God's word emphasizes as necessary to salvation and they conclude that is all that we need.

* Some read about our need for the **grace of God**, and they conclude we are saved by "grace alone."

* Others read about the importance of ***Jesus' death and blood***, so they conclude "Jesus' blood is all we need."

* Some read about the need for ***love***, and they conclude all you need to do is to treat others with a loving manner.

* Others read about out need for ***faith***, so they believe we are saved by "faith only."

* Some say they lead a ***good moral life,*** so they think that is enough.

* Some even think they have been ***baptized*** or they are ***members of a church***, so they think nothing more is needed.

The purpose of this study is to examine what the Bible says is necessary to our salvation and consider whether any one thing alone saves us.

Surely all the things we just mentioned are important. But does any one of them by itself alone save us? Or do we need some combination of things to be saved? Consider what God's word says.

A List of Things Essential to Salvation

God's Provisions

The Father, Son, and Holy Spirit have all been active in our salvation. They all have done things necessary to our salvation. Consider some specifics:

Grace and mercy

Titus 2:11 — For the **grace** of God that brings salvation has appeared to all men.

So, God's grace is essential to our salvation.

(Titus 3:5; Romans 3:24; Ephesians 2:8,9; 2 Timothy 1:9; Ephesians 1:7; Acts 15:11)

Death and blood of Jesus

Romans 5:9,10 — We have been justified by His **blood**, reconciled by His **death**.

Ephesians 1:7 — We have redemption through His **blood**, the forgiveness of sins.

Surely we cannot be saved without the blood of Jesus.

(Hebrews 10:10; 1 Corinthians 15:3; 1 John 1:7; Hebrews 9:14,22; Romans 3:25; 1 Peter 1:18,19; Revelation 1:5)

The resurrection of Jesus

1 Corinthians 15:17 — And if Christ is not **risen**, your faith *is* futile; you are still in your sins!

Without the resurrection, Jesus' death would have been a victory for Satan!

(Romans 5:10; Hebrews 7:25; 1 Peter 3:21)

The gospel, God's word

Romans 1:16 — The **gospel** is the power of God unto salvation.

1 Peter 1:23-25 — We are born again by the seed, which is **God's word**.

Acts 11:14 — Peter told Cornelius **words** whereby he would be saved.

(James 1:18,21; 1 Corinthians 15:1,2; John 8:31,32)

These blessings and provisions from God are all essential in order to make salvation available to us. Without them, we could never have achieved salvation by our human ability.

But note that we have already learned that a number of things are essential to our salvation. We are not saved by any one of these things alone.

Man's Response

Some people believe that God's provisions are all we need, so **nothing** is required on man's part. However, God's provisions are freely offered to all men (Titus 2:11; 1 Timothy 2:4,6; Hebrews 2:9; 2 Peter 3:9; etc.). But not all people will ultimately be saved (Matthew 7:13,14; 25:31-46). So there must be something in the life of each individual that determines whether or not he will receive God's forgiveness. What is it?

Hearing and learning God's word

John 6:44,45 — No man can come to Jesus without **hearing**, **learning**, and being **taught**.

Romans 10:17 — Faith comes by **hearing** the word of God.

We cannot be saved until we learn from God's word what He requires. The Spirit does not work directly on man's heart to lead to salvation, but works through the word (Ephesians 6:17).

(1 Corinthians 1:21; 2 Timothy 3:16,17; John 8:31,32; Matthew 13:23; Romans 1:16; 10:13,14; Mark 16:15,16; Acts 8:26,29,35; 9:6; 11:14; 18:8; Luke 6:46-49; 11:28; 2 Thessalonians 2:14; Revelation 3:20)

Love

Matthew 22:36-39 – **Love** for God and others are the greatest two commands.

1 Corinthians 16:22 – Anyone who does not **love** the Lord will be accursed.

Can we be saved without love for God?

(1 Corinthians 13:1-3 1 John 4:7,8)

Faith

Romans 5:1 — We are justified by ***faith***.

Hebrews 11:6 — Without ***faith*** it is impossible to please Him, for he who comes to God must believe that He is, and that He is a rewarder of those who diligently seek Him.

The Bible describes different kinds and degrees of faith. Some believe God exists and Jesus is the Savior, but will not obey Him. This is not saving faith (James 2:19; John 12:41,42). We will learn that saving faith leads one to **obey** Jesus (Galatians 5:6; James 2:14-26; Hebrews 11).

(Romans 10:9,10; Galatians 3:26; John 3:16; 8:24; Mark 16:16; Acts 16:31; Ephesians 2:8; Hebrews 10:39; Hope — Romans 8:24; Love — 1 John 4:7,8; Galatians 5:6; 1 Corinthians 13:1-3; 16:22)

Repentance

2 Corinthians 7:10 — Godly sorrow produces **repentance** leading to salvation.

Acts 2:38 — **Repent** and be baptized for the remission of sins.

Repentance is a change of mind in which one determines to turn from sin and *do* what God says (Matt. 21:28,29). Without this decision, God will not save us.

(Luke 13:3,5; 24:47; Acts 17:30; Acts 2:38; 3:19; 5:31; 20:21; 2 Peter 3:9)

Obedience to God's commands

To be forgiven, we must follow through on our repentance and *do* what God says. Many people will agree with everything to this point, but deny we must *do* anything. But note:

Hebrews 5:9 — Jesus is the author of eternal salvation to all who **obey** Him.

Romans 6:17,18 — When we **obey** from the heart the teaching delivered, we are then made free from sin.

1 Peter 1:22 — We purify our souls in **obeying** the truth.

Acts 10:34,35 — Whoever fears God and **works** righteousness is accepted by Him.

It is simply not true that nothing man does is necessary to salvation.

(Matthew 7:21-27; 22:36-39; John 14:15,21-24; Acts 3:20-23; Romans 2:6-10; Hebrews 10:39; 11:8,30; Galatians 5:6; 2 Thessalonians 1:8,9; James 2:14-26; 1 John 5:3; 2:3-6)

Confession of Christ

Romans 10:9,10 — With the heart man believes to righteousness, and with the mouth **confession** is made to salvation.

Here is a physical act that must be done with the mouth to be saved: one must confess. To deny we must do anything to be saved is to deny confession is necessary.

(Matthew 10:32; 16:15-18; John 1:49; 4:42; 9:35-38; 11:27: 12:42,43; Acts 8:36-38; 1 Timothy 6:12,13; 1 John 4:15)

Baptism (immersion in water)

Many deny this step is necessary to be saved. Yet notice what the Bible teaches:

Mark 16:16 — He who believes and is **baptized** will be saved; but he who does not believe will be condemned. Is a person saved before or without baptism? No more so than he is saved before or without faith!

Acts 2:38 — Repent and be **baptized** for the remission of sins. Are sins remitted before or without baptism? No more so than they are remitted before or without repentance! Peter was here talking to people in sin, telling them how to receive remission. The fact he told them to **repent** makes that clear. But to receive remission, they also needed to be baptized.

Acts 22:16 — And now why are you waiting? Arise and be **baptized**, and wash away your sins, calling on the name of the Lord. Were sins washed away before baptism or as a result of it? A person is in sin until he has been baptized!

1 Peter 3:21 — ***Baptism*** doth also now save us.

The Bible says baptism is necessary to salvation just as clearly as it does the other conditions. The power to forgive is not in the water, or in faith, repentance, or confession. The power is in Jesus' blood, but that power benefits an individual only when he meets the conditions.

(Romans 6:3-7; Galatians 3:26,27)

Faithfulness, endurance

Matthew 10:22 — He who ***endures*** to the end will be saved.

Revelation 2:10 — Be ***faithful*** until death, and I will give you the crown of life.

Again, some folks teach "once saved, always saved," denying faithfulness is necessary. Yet these verses affirm it is just as essential as the other conditions.

(1 Corinthians 15:1,2,58; Matthew 28:20; Titus 2:11,12; 1 John 2:1-6)

Church membership

Again people say, "The church doesn't save you. Christ saves you." So they conclude we don't need to be members of the church to be saved. But the Bible says:

Acts 2:47 — The Lord added to the church daily those who were being saved. The church does not save, but those who are saved are in the church.

Acts 20:28 — Jesus purchased the ***church*** with His blood (that which saves us).

Ephesians 5:23,25 — Jesus is Savior of the ***body*** (church), and gave Himself for the ***church***. How can one be saved if He is not part of that which Jesus died to save?

So, the Scriptures show that there are many things God did to make salvation available to man, and there are several things each person must do to receive the salvation God offers.

Proper Applications

People often misunderstand salvation because they ***isolate*** certain passages from the total context of God's will. They pick a few things the Bible says, and rest their salvation on those things, ignoring other things the Bible elsewhere states are essential.

I once heard a preacher tell a man, "The only passage you need to know to be saved is John 3:16." Then what purpose is served by the rest of the Bible? And if other passages say something else is essential but I neglect it, how can I be saved? Consider some applications.

Some Say We Are "Saved by Grace Alone."

This is found in many denominational creeds. Universalists conclude from this that everyone will be saved.

But God's grace is available to all. If grace is all we need, then all will be saved! But we know some will be lost, so something must be wrong with the doctrine of salvation by grace alone!

The problem is that the doctrine ignores other things the Bible says are essential to salvation. If we take only the verses that show we need grace, we will reach conclusions that contradict other passages. The solution is to realize that, although the Bible says we are saved by grace, it never says we are saved by grace *alone*. Instead it says other things are also needed.

Unfortunately, even though grace has been extended to all, some folks will be lost because they fail to meet the other conditions.

Others Say All We Need Is the Death of Jesus.

They may say, "Jesus blood is all you need. You don't have to do anything." Again, this leads to a contradiction in Bible teaching. Jesus died for everyone, just like God's grace is for everyone (Heb. 2:9; 1 Tim. 2:4,6). If Jesus' death is all we need, then everyone will be saved. But that contradicts the Bible teaching that not everyone will be saved.

Again, the problem is that people ignore other things the Bible says are essential. The solution is to realize that, though the Bible says we are saved by Jesus' death, it does not say His death *alone* saves us, with nothing else needed on our part. Instead it shows that other things are necessary.

Unfortunately, although Jesus died to save all men, some will be lost because they will not meet the conditions.

Others Think They Will Be Saved Just Because They Are Good Moral People.

When told they need to obey the gospel, they appeal to their good moral life and think that is all they need. Again, this contradicts Bible teaching, since the Bible describes good moral people like Cornelius who were lost (Acts 10:1ff; 11:14).

The problem is that people are ignoring other things the Bible says are essential. The solution is to realize that the Bible does say that a good moral life is necessary — this is part of faithful living. But it does not say that a good moral life *alone* will save us. Instead it says other things are necessary.

Unfortunately, many good moral people will be lost because they failed to meet the conditions to be forgiven of their sins.

Many Believe They Will Be Saved by "Faith Alone."

When told they need to be baptized and live a faithful life, they say that's not necessary as long as one believes in Jesus as His personal Savior. Again, this contradicts the Bible, since it describes many people who believed in Jesus but were not saved (James 2:19; John 12:42,43; Acts 22:1-16; Matt. 7:21-27).

The problem is that people ignore the Bible teaching about other things that are necessary to salvation. If faith is all we need, then we do not even need repentance and confession, let alone baptism! Some may say these are part of faith, but the Bible sometimes lists them separately from faith just like it does baptism (Rom. 10:9,10).

The solution is to realize that the Bible says we are saved by faith, but it never says we are saved by faith *only*. Instead, it expressly denies we are saved by faith only (James 2:24), and it states other things that are necessary.

Unfortunately there are many people who have faith in Jesus, who yet will be lost because they have not met the other conditions (see examples above).

Some Think We Are Saved by Baptism Alone.

Some people baptize babies to save them from original sin. Others act as though faithful living is not necessary because they have been baptized. This contradicts the Bible teaching that people must believe, repent, and confess before they are baptized (Mark 16:16; Acts 2:38; etc.), and that many baptized people become unfaithful and were lost (Galatians 5:4; Hebrews 10:26ff; Acts 8:12-24).

The problem is that people are ignoring the other things the Bible says are necessary. The solution is to realize that, though baptism is necessary to salvation, the Bible nowhere says we are saved by baptism *only*. Instead it says other things are needed.

Unfortunately, there are people who have been baptized, who will yet be lost because they have not met the other conditions of salvation.

Conclusion

Acts 3:22,23 says we must give heed to *all* things that Jesus teaches.

Salvation may be compared to following a recipe or following instructions to assemble a product for which "some assembly is required." To have the desired result, it is not enough to follow one step and ignore the rest. One must take the instructions as a whole.

Have you followed all that the Lord requires to be forgiven of sins? Are you living the faithful life that He also requires after your sins have been forgiven?

(James 2:10; Revelation 22:18,19; Acts 20:27; Matthew 28:20; 4:4-7)

The Importance of Hearing the Gospel

Introduction:
What kind of message would you consider to be really good news: the birth of a baby? A promotion or pay raise at work? The victory of a sports team? What constitutes good news varies according to the person.

In this lesson we want to study the most important kind of good news there is: the good news of the gospel of salvation through Jesus. We want to consider:
* What does it mean to "hear the gospel"?
* What effects does the gospel have in man's salvation?
* Can a person be saved without hearing the gospel?

What Does It Mean To "Hear the Gospel?"

What Does It Mean to "Hear"?

The word "hear" has different shades of meaning in different contexts.

1. To notice or perceive a sound

It is possible to be aware of a sound regardless of whether or not you understand the meaning of it.

Matthew 13:19 — The wayside soil in the parable of the sower represents those who **hear** the word but **do not understand** it, so the devil takes it away.

2. To understand the meaning of a sound (especially of words)

Matthew 13:13-16 — Jesus said of Jews, "**Hearing** they **hear** not, neither do they understand" because they closed their eyes and had ears dull of hearing. They heard (perceived the sound), but did not hear (understand the meaning). (John 6:60)

You may call someone and they say, "What did you say? I did not hear you." Obviously, they perceived the sound or they would not have responded. But they did not understand what you said.

3. To respond favorably to the message (to obey)

When a child is told what to do but does not obey, the parent may say: "Did you **hear** what I said? Why don't you **listen** to me?" He perceived the sound and understood, but did not obey.

2 Kings 17:13-15 — God rebuked Israel because they would not **hear** His law, but stiffened their necks and rejected His statutes, etc. They had been told God's word by the prophets, but simply would not **obey**.

Matthew 18:15-17 — If a brother sins against another and is rebuked, he must **hear** his brother so they can be reconciled. If he will not hear the brother or several brethren, or the church, he is chastened. It is not enough for him to perceive the sound or even to understand what is said, but he must respond favorably. (John 18:37; 1 John 4:6)

In this sense, "hear" is like "believe." It can have a limited meaning or a more general meaning. In the general sense, it refers to all that man does in responding to the gospel call to be saved.

(John 8:47,43; 10:3,8,27; Acts 3:22,23; Luke 16:29-31; 10:16; Matthew 17:5)

What Is the "Gospel"?

Gospel means "good news," especially the good news of salvation through Jesus.

It includes the entire New Testament message of God's will for man today.

Facts

The gospel includes information about the works God has done to provide salvation.

1 Corinthians 15:1-5 — The gospel by which we are saved involves the death, burial, resurrection, and appearances of Jesus. This is the basic foundation on which the whole gospel rests, but it is not all there is to the gospel.

Conditions

The gospel includes instructions that tell people how we must respond in order to receive the benefits of the gospel.

Mark 16:15,16 — Jesus commanded His disciples to preach the gospel to every creature. Specifically, they should preach that people must believe and be baptized to be saved.

(Acts 20:21,24)

All New Testament Instructions

The gospel includes all God's will for us, including instructions about faithful living as Christians.

1 Timothy 1:8-11 — Many sins are listed; all are contrary to sound doctrine "according to the gospel." So, the gospel includes warnings against such sins.

Some people claim "gospel" is different from "doctrine."

They say that the "gospel" is the first principles about how to become a Christian, but "doctrine" is teachings about how to live the Christian life. Why make such a distinction? Because they believe error in "gospel" separates us from God, but doctrinal error does not. In this way, they seek to promote fellowship and "unity" with people who practice error about worship, church organization, etc.: "unity in diversity."

But note:

Instructions to Christians are called "gospel."

1 Timothy 1:8-11 — Various sins are contrary to the "doctrine according to the gospel." Doctrine and gospel here refer to the same thing, and both refer to things that are surely not first principles of becoming a Christian.

Romans 1:7,15 — Paul was ready to preach the **gospel** to saints. When speaking to Christians, Paul never limited himself to first principles of how to become a Christian, yet his teaching is called "gospel." (Galatians 2:11-14; Romans 16:25,26; 2 Corinthians 9:13)

Instructions to non-Christians were called "doctrine" (teaching).

Romans 6:17,18 — People, who were slaves to sin, were made free from sin and became servants of righteousness by obeying the "form of **doctrine**."

Hebrews 6:2 — The "first principles of Christ" are called "**doctrine**."

Just as there are different terms that refer to God, different terms for the church, or for Christians, etc., so "gospel" and "doctrine" are just different terms for the New Testament message. Each term just emphasizes different aspects of the message. "Gospel" emphasizes the fact the message produces joy. "Doctrine" emphasizes that the message must be taught and studied for one to know God's will.

This does not mean one must understand the whole gospel before he can become a Christian (Matthew 28:19,20). But all New Testament teaching is gospel.

(Other passages disproving the gospel/doctrine distinction: Acts 13:12; 4:2; 5:21,28,42; 20:20,21,24,27; 17:19; 28:31; Hebrews 5:12; Titus 1:9,10.)

(Passages showing that salvation requires having proper "doctrine," not false doctrine: Romans 16:17,18; Matthew 15:9,13; 1 Timothy 4:16; 2 John 9-11.)

(Other terms for the gospel message: "word" — 1 Peter 1:22-25; 1 Corinthians 15:1ff; Romans 10:8ff; Ephesians 1:13; Colossians 1:5; Acts 15:7; "truth" — 1 Peter 1:22-25; Ephesians 1:13; 2 Corinthians 4:1-6; Galatians 2:5,14; Colossians 1:5,6; "the faith" — Philippians 1:27; Colossians 1:23; Acts 14:21,22; Galatians 1:23. Note that studying these terms further would confirm that these terms for the "gospel" also refer to the "doctrine.")

What Effects Does Hearing the Gospel Produce?

What is the gospel designed to accomplish in our lives? What role does it play in our salvation? Why should we hear it and strive to understand it? Why should we teach it to others?

The Gospel Can Produce Knowledge and Understanding of God's Will.

The gospel will produce this effect on those who have receptive hearts.

Matthew 13:23 — In the parable of the sower, the good soil represents those who **hear and understand** the word and bring forth good fruit.

John 6:44,45 — We cannot come to Jesus unless we are taught, hear, and learn.

(Matthew 11:29; John 8:32; Acts 10:33; 11:14; 8:30; 13:7,44; 19:2,5,10; Ephesians 3:3-5; 5:17; 1:18; 4:20,21; John 18:37; Colossians 1:9,23,5,6; 2 Timothy 2:7; 3:16,17; 4:1-4; Acts 17:11; Mark 12:37; Luke 10:39,42; 15:1; 19:48; 21:38; 5:1)

Yet, those who resist the gospel when they hear it, may still misunderstand.

Matthew 13:13-16 — Some hear but don't understand because they close their ears and have gross hearts. Many do not want to deny their own desires, change their way of living, or sacrifice their own will to serve God. These will reject the teaching, and may not even understand it.

In which category are you and I?

(John 8:47; Luke 10:16; 1 John 4:6; Hebrews 5:11; 2 Timothy 3:7; Matthew 11:15; 17:5; 10:14; etc.)

The Gospel Can Produce Faith in Christ and His Will.

The gospel will produce this effect in those who have receptive hearts.

John 4:41,42 — The Samaritans believed because they heard Jesus' word for themselves and knew He was the Savior of the world.

Acts 18:8 — Many of the Corinthians, hearing, believed and were baptized.

Romans 10:17 — So faith comes by hearing, and hearing by the word of God.

(Acts 15:7; 4:4; 8:6,12; Ephesians 1:13; John 20:30,31; Mark 16:15,16; John 5:24; Luke 16:29-31; Acts 24:24; 2 Thessalonians 2:13,14)

Again, some who hear will resist the teaching and refuse to believe.

2 Thessalonians 2:10-12 — Some believe not the truth but believe a lie, because they don't **love** the truth but have pleasure in unrighteousness. Some don't want to admit their error or change their lives. The gospel is designed so that such people will not believe.

Hebrews 4:2 — Speaking of Israel's hope of entering the promised land, it is written: "The gospel was preached to us as well as to them; but the word which they heard did not profit them, not being mixed with faith in those who heard it." They heard but did not have true faith. So, we today each have a choice about our response.

Note that people reject the gospel, not because it is not true, nor because there is not adequate evidence for it, but because of attitude problems in their own hearts.

What is your attitude toward gospel truth? Are you willing to believe and accept it, even when it contradicts your former ideas? Are you willing to make the necessary changes to be right, or will you reject it because you are too much involved in things that please you?

(Hebrews 3:7; Luke 8:12; Mark 16:16; Romans 10:16-18; John 12:47,48)

The Gospel Can Motivate Obedience to God's Word.

The gospel will produce this effect on those who have receptive hearts.

Luke 11:28 — "...blessed are those who hear the word of God and keep it!"

Matthew 13:23 — The good soil refers to those who hear and understand the word and **bear fruit** (do the good works God requires).

Acts 2:37 — When the Jews on Pentecost heard the gospel, they were pricked in their hearts and asked what they should **do**. Hearing the gospel motivated them to want to obey.

(Acts 18:8; 8:6,12; 19:2,5; 1 Peter 1:22-25; Luke 8:21; Philippians 4:9; 1 Timothy 4:16; Hebrews 2:1-3; Revelation 1:3; 3:3; 2 Timothy 3:14; Titus 3:14; Mark 16:15,16; Philippians 1:27; Luke 16:29-31; Romans 10:13,14; 2 Timothy 1:13; 1 Corinthians 4:15)

Again, some people reject the message and refuse to obey.

Acts 5:33 — When the Jewish council heard what the apostles preached, they were furious and took counsel to kill them. Note the contrast to the Jews on Pentecost: the same basic message produced completely opposite effects, because of the attitudes of the hearers.

Luke 6:46-49 — Those who hear and obey Jesus' word are like a wise builder, whose house survives the storm because it is built on a good foundation. Those who hear but don't obey are building on the sand. Which one are you?

James 1:22-25 — We must be doers of the word, not just hearers. If we do not do what the word says, we are like a man who looks in a mirror but does nothing about the problems he sees in his appearance. What good does it do to look, if we do not correct the faults we find?

God created His word to produce understanding, faith, and obedience in the lives of those who have receptive hearts. But He also created each person with the power to choose. The gospel does not violate that power; it appeals to it. God designed the word to attract those who have open hearts but to repel those who are determined to continue in sin.

In which category are you and I?

(Acts 7:54; 3:22,23; 2 Thessalonians 1:7-9; 1 Peter 4:17,18)

How Essential Is Hearing the Gospel?

All the effects produced by hearing the gospel are essential to salvation. But could these effects be produced any other way?

Some people claim the Holy Spirit works directly on the heart of sinners, separate and apart from the word, to make the sinner believe. The sinner is saved from His sins directly by the Spirit, without study of God's word (or perhaps in conjunction with study, but the Spirit must act in addition to the teaching of the Scriptures).

Some say, "I was saved while driving down the road (or doing dishes, etc.). The Holy Spirit suddenly overwhelmed me, and I knew I was saved." This is called a "better felt than told" salvation experience or "irresistible work of the Spirit."

The Bible Teaches the Only Way to Be Saved Is to Study, Learn, and Obey What the Gospel Says about Salvation.

John 6:44,45 — The only way to come to Jesus is to be **taught**. We must **hear and learn** from the Father. One is not saved by a direct operation on the heart apart from the word. You can't come without being taught, hearing, and learning.

2 Thessalonians 2:14 — We are called to obtain the glory in Jesus. How are we called? "He called you through our **gospel**."

Romans 1:16 — The gospel is the power of God unto salvation.

Nowhere does the Bible speak of one who is not a Christian being saved directly by the Holy Spirit apart from the word. Rather, the Bible teaches that, to be saved one must learn what the gospel teaches and obey it.

(Romans 10:13-17; 2 Corinthians 5:18-20; 4:7)

Examples of Conversion Show that People Must Receive God's Word through an Inspired Human Agent to Be Saved.

God never saved anyone without obedience to the conditions of the gospel (hearing, believing, and obeying in confession and baptism). And no one ever learned the conditions of salvation in any way other than through an inspired human agent.

This does not mean you must hear the message from someone living today. But remember that the Bible came to us through human agents — the inspired men who wrote it. Whether people learned the gospel directly from the lips of inspired men in the first century, or whether we today learn it through the message written in the Bible by the inspired men, either way people must learn through the human agency of inspired men.

Acts 8:26,29,35 — The Spirit directed Philip to preach to the eunuch. Why didn't the Spirit just operate directly on the eunuch's heart? If it is true that the Holy Spirit operates directly on the hearts of men, why didn't the Spirit just directly preach the message to the eunuch? Obviously, God did not choose to work that way. He sent an inspired man.

Acts 9:6 — Saul was traveling to Damascus to persecute Christians. To convince Saul that Jesus had been raised and to qualify Saul to be an apostle, Jesus personally appeared to Him. But when Saul asked what Jesus wanted him to do, Jesus would not tell him! He said to enter the city and it would be **told** him what he must do. Then the Lord sent Ananias to tell Saul to be baptized (22:6).

Why did Saul have to be **told** anything? Why didn't Jesus tell him? If the Holy Spirit operates directly on the heart of the sinner, why did God send Ananias to Saul? The answer is that God requires sinners to learn the gospel through inspired men.

Acts 11:14 — Cornelius saw an angel who told him to send for Peter (10:22,33) who would tell him **words** whereby he and his house could be saved. Why did he have to be **told words**? Why didn't the angel tell him the words? Why send for Peter? God's will is that people must learn how to be saved through inspired men.

Romans 10:13,14,17 — Can you call on Jesus and be saved without believing? It is impossible (Hebrews 11:6; John 8:24). Can you believe without hearing the words of a preacher? Equally impossible! Faith comes by **hearing** God's word — no other way. The "preachers" referred to here are not men living today, but the inspired men who revealed the New Testament.

God never told the conditions of salvation to anyone by means of a revelation directly to them from the Holy Spirit or by acting directly on the sinner's heart apart from the word. God decreed that people learn the truth by being taught the inspired message of the gospel by means of inspired men. Then the people must choose whether to believe and obey.

In the first century, some people learned the truth by words spoken to them by inspired men. Later in the first century and since that time, people learn by the words written by the inspired men of the first century (in the gospel).

Are you in sin? If so, you can be saved only by learning what is recorded by inspired men in God's written word.

Are you saved from sin? If so, will you help other people learn what is written in the word?

(Matthew 13:13-17; 1 Timothy 4:16; 2 Timothy 1:13; 2:2; 2 Corinthians 5:18; 4:7; 1 John 4:6)

Conclusion

Revelation 3:20 — Man's salvation involves both God's side and man's side. Jesus died for us, and now He stands at the door of our hearts knocking. He asks you to receive Him and the salvation He offers. But He will not force His way in. You must make the choice to accept His salvation.

You must hear His voice.

God will not operate directly on your heart apart from the word. His voice speaks to you through the Scriptures (2 Timothy 3:16,17). You must listen or be lost.

You must open the door.

You must give the proper response to what you hear by obeying the conditions of the message. As in the examples in the Bible, you do this by believing in Jesus, repenting of sins, confessing Jesus, and being baptized. Then you must continue to live a faithful life, learning and obeying all that the gospel teaches as God's will for your life.

The choice is yours. What response will you give?

What Must We Believe?

Introduction:
Many Scriptures teach that we are saved by faith. But does it follow, just because a person has "faith," that he will be saved? Is it possible to have a faith that does not save?
(Hebrews 10:39; 11:1,4-8,17,30; Romans 1:16; 4:19-21; 5:1,2; 10:9,10,13-17; Galatians 5:6; 2 Corinthians 5:7; James 2:14-26; John 1:12; 3:15-18; 8:24; 20:30,31; Mark 16:15,16)

There are different kinds of faith.

Many people think others are saved because they "believe," yet they seem to have little concern about what they believe. This is especially confusing in the case of those who claim we are saved by "faith alone."

* Some think it's enough to "believe in god": some concept of a Supreme Being or some "force" that operates the universe.

* Others claim Hindus and Buddhists will be saved because they "believe in god": many gods worshiped by images, etc.

* Others claim Jews and Muslims will be saved because "they believe in the same God you do."

* Many liberal modernists don't believe in Jesus' miracles or Deity or resurrection, yet they claim they "believe in Jesus": He existed and was a great teacher, maybe even a prophet.

* Many denominationalists disbelieve much of what Jesus taught yet they think they will be saved because they believe He is the Christ, the Son of God, who died to save them from their sins.

The purpose of this study is to consider what the Bible says we must believe to be saved.

Titus 2:2 – It is important to be "sound in faith." "Sound" means wholesome or spiritually healthy. There is faith that leads to spiritual life and health, but there is also faith that leads to spiritual disease and death.

There are different kinds of faith, like there are different kinds of love. A person may have love, but he may love the wrong thing. So a person may have "faith," but he may believe the wrong thing.

So, what is the content of faith that saves? Our intent here is not to make a complete itemized list. Instead, we seek to show that what we believe matters, so we can avoid many false conceptions of faith.

What must one believe to be saved?

Believe in God.

What are some things one must believe about God to be saved?

We Must Believe in God's Existence.

Hebrews 11:6 – Without faith it is impossible to please God. We must believe that He *is*. Note that it is not enough to believe that there *was* or has been a god who created the universe. Some believe "God is dead." We must believe in His continued existence: God *is.*

Some might think this general belief in a god would be enough. But there is more.

(1 Peter 1:21; John 5:24; 14:1; 12:44; 2 Chronicles 20:20; Acts 16:34; 1 Thessalonians 1:8)

We Must Believe in God's Works (Miracles).

Psalms 78:32,33 – God punished Israel because they sinned and did not believe in His wondrous *works* (miracles).

Hebrews 11:3 – By faith we understand the worlds were framed by the word of God. True faith believes God spoke the world into existence.

To have a saving faith we must believe, not just that God exists, but that He has done miracles in history.

(Romans 4:24; 1 Peter 1:21)

We Must Believe in God's Character and Power.

We will not itemize everything, but note a few specifics:

John 6:69 – Peter believed Jesus is the Christ the Son of the *living* God.

1 Corinthians 2:5 – We should have faith in the *power* of God. God is all-powerful, ruling the entire universe.

1 John 4:16 – We have known and believe the *love* God has for us.

New Agers, Hindus, and others may believe in some impersonal power or "force" (as in Star Wars), but this is not a proper faith. God is a living God who loves His creatures. He possesses the characteristics of individual personality.

(Colossians 2:12; Daniel 6:20-23; Psalms 27:13; 78:22; Matthew 6:30; 8:26)

We Must Believe in One True God.

2 Kings 17:10-14 – When Israel worshiped other gods, God said they did not believe in the Lord their God. Like many idol worshipers

today, doubtless they would have claimed to believe in God: they believe in Him as one among many gods. But to God this meant they did not believe in Him! (Deuteronomy 32:16-20)

Isaiah 43:10-12 – To truly believe in God, we must know and believe that there is no other god before or after Him.

James 2:19 – Even the demons believe there is one God, but are they saved?

What about the faith of Hindus, Buddhists, and others who believe in many gods or who worship idols or nature or the earth or some god other than the God of the Bible? Even demons know better than that! They know there is one true God and they know who that God is. But that faith is not enough to save them. So how can anyone be saved with a lesser faith?

Believing in God involves much more than many people realize.

Believe in Jesus.

We Must Believe in Jesus.

John 14:1 – Jesus said: "You believe in God; believe also in Me." Belief in God requires us to believe in Jesus.

John 8:24 – If you believe not that I am He, you shall die in your sins.

To be saved, we must believe in Jesus. But it is not enough to have just any kind of faith. As with faith in God, there are specific things we must believe.

(John 3:15,16,18,36; 5:38,46; 6:29,40,97; 13:19; Acts 9:42; 10:43; 11:17; 14:23; 18:8; 19:4; 20:21; Romans 3:22; 9:33; Galatians 2:16,20; 3:26; Ephesians 1:15; Colossians 1:4; 1 Timothy 1:16; 3:16; 2 Timothy 3:15; Philemon 5; 1 John 3:23; 5:1,5,10,13)

We Must Believe in Jesus' Character and Works.

John 10:38 – Jesus said people should believe His works, so they would know and believe that He and His Father are in one another. To believe in Jesus we must believe His works: His miracles.

John 11:27 – Martha said she believed Jesus to be the Christ, the Son of God. "Christ" means He is the anointed One: the ruler God sent to be spiritual King over His people. But what does it mean to believe He is the Son of God?

Matthew 16:13-17 – Some people believed Jesus was a great prophet like Old Testament prophets, but that was not enough. Peter confessed Him to be the Christ, the Son of God, and Jesus said this is what the Father had revealed. To believe Jesus is the Son of God requires us to believe He is more than a mere man, more even than a great prophet.

John 20:27-31 – Thomas confessed Jesus to be His Lord and God. Jesus pronounced a blessing on all others who believe the same thing. On the basis of the written record we should believe that He is the Christ, the Son of God, and by believing we have life in His name.

To believe Jesus is the Son of God is to believe He is Lord and God. He partakes of the nature of God, because He was not just a man. He was God in the flesh (John 1:1-18).

Muslims, modernists, and some Jews claim to believe in Jesus as a prophet and teacher, but they say He was just a great man, like Moses. Some of them deny His miracles, others deny He was the Son of God. We are sometimes told that such people are true believers, because "they believe in Jesus." But their faith is not a sufficient faith.

To have faith that leads to eternal life, we must believe Jesus is more than just a man. He is the Christ, the Son of God, God in the flesh.

(John 17:8; 11:42; 16:27,30; 17:21; 6:69; 9:35-38; 14:10,11; Acts 8:37; 16:31)

We Must Believe in Jesus as Our Sacrifice and Savior.

John 4:42 – The Samaritans confessed that they believed Jesus is the Christ, the Savior of the world.

1 Corinthians 15:1-8 – Paul declared the gospel by which people will be saved, unless they believe in vain. The basics of this gospel are Jesus' death, burial, resurrection, and appearances.

Again, Muslims and others believe Jesus was a great man and great prophet, but they deny He was crucified as the sacrifice to save us from our sins. Such is not a true faith. To really believe in Jesus, we must believe the only way to salvation is through His crucifixion (John 14:6; Acts 4:12).

(1 Thessalonians 4:14; Acts 15:11)

We Must Believe in Jesus' Resurrection.

1 Corinthians 15:1-8 – In order to be saved people must believe the gospel teaching that Jesus not only died but also arose from the dead.

Romans 10:9,10 – To be saved we must believe that God raised Jesus from the dead, and we must be willing to confess Him to be Lord. We are not saved by just some general "faith in Jesus." We must specifically believe in His death for our salvation and in His resurrection.

John 20:27-29 – Thomas had said he would not believe in Jesus' resurrection till He saw for himself (verses 24-26). Jesus appeared to the apostles and told Thomas to touch his hands and side. "Do not be unbelieving, but believing." The KJV says, "Do not be faithless..." So those who doubt Jesus' resurrection are "faithless." They are "unbelievers."

All around us are people who claim to believe in Jesus, but they doubt or deny that He was the Son of God, was God in the flesh, did miracles, died as the sacrifice to save us from sins, and/or arose from the dead. Many people tell us that these people are believers and God will accept them. Such people may have a sort of faith, but according to the gospel they do not have a true faith. They need to become true believers to be saved.

(1 Thessalonians 4:14; Mark 16:14)

Believe in God's Word.

Let us consider even more about the content of faith.

General Statements Regarding Believing God's Word

Believe God's word/commands.

Psalms 106:12,24,25 – When Israel had crossed the Red Sea, they believed God's **words**. But when they came to enter the Promised Land they did not believe His words and did not heed His voice.

Psalms 119:66 – I believe your commandments.

To truly believe in God we must believe what God says, especially what He commands us to do. Those who reject God's commands do not really believe in Him.

(John 12:47,48; Genesis 15:5,6 cf. Romans 4:3,18,19,20; Galatians 3:6)

Believe the prophets.

2 Chronicles 20:20 – Jehoshaphat called on the people to believe in the Lord and believe His prophets, so they would prosper.

1 John 4:1 – Do not believe false prophets, but put them to the test. Not only does it matter what we believe, it matters what we do **not** believe.

Many people believe some things about God and Jesus. But a true faith requires us to believe the message God sent by His inspired teachers and to reject teachings that contradict God's inspired word.

(Acts 8:12; 2 Thessalonians 1:10; Exodus 14:31; 4:1-9; Jonah 3:5; Matthew 21:32; Luke 24:25; 1 Corinthians 15:11)

Believe the Scriptures.

John 2:22 – The disciples believed the **scriptures** and the **word** Jesus said. Faith is not just believing what Jesus did and who He was. It requires believing what He taught!

John 5:46,47 – Those who do not believe Moses' **writings** will not believe Jesus' **word**. Proper faith requires believing both the Scriptures and the teachings of Jesus.

The message of God's inspired prophets is recorded in the Scriptures. To believe in God, we must believe the message He inspired, which we find today in the Bible. Those who disbelieve what the Bible tells us to do to receive eternal life have an improper faith.
(Acts 24:14)

Believe the truth.

John 8:45-47 – Jesus said these people were not of God because they did not believe the **truth** that Jesus told them: they did not hear God's **words.**

2 Thessalonians 2:11-13 – We are chosen for salvation through belief of the **truth.** Those who have pleasure in unrighteousness will not believe the truth but will believe a lie and will be condemned.

Again, it matters, not just what we believe, but what we do **not** believe. Those who do not believe truth but believe lies will be condemned.
(1 Timothy 4:1-3)

Believe the gospel.

Mark 1:15 – Jesus taught: Repent and believe the **gospel.**

1 Corinthians 15:1-8 – The people believed the **gospel** that Paul **preached** (verse 11).

The gospel is the message of God for today, revealed by Jesus and His inspired apostles and prophets, and recorded in the New Testament. People may claim to believe in Jesus, but if they do not believe His words, they do not truly believe.
(Mark 16:15,16; Philippians 1:27; John 11:25,26; Acts 15:7; 26:27; 27:25; Romans 10:14,16,17; 1 Corinthians 1:21; 1 Thessalonians 2:13; 1 Timothy 4:6; 6:10; 5:12; 6:21; 2 Timothy 1:12,13; 1 Peter 2:6,7)

Specific Teachings to Believe

We will not attempt to list every specific point we must believe, but let us consider enough to show that it matters what we believe.

Obedience

Deuteronomy 1:26-33 – When Israel refused to obey God's command, Moses said they did not believe **God.** A true faith requires us to believe that obedience is necessary to please God.
(Numbers 14:1-11; 20:12; Deuteronomy 9:33; Hebrews 3:19; 4:2)

2 Kings 17:10-14 – God sent Israel into captivity because they worshiped idols and would not keep the commands sent by the prophets. They did not **believe** God. When people do not think obedience is necessary to please God, they do not believe God!

Hebrews 11 – Old Testament people illustrate the kind of faith we need to be saved (10:39). In every case, their faith led them to obey God. Noah built the ark (verse 7). Abraham obeyed to go to the land God would show him (verse 8). Israel encircled Jericho seven days (verse 30), etc.

All these people believed that they needed to obey God to receive His reward, but this is the kind of faith we need to be saved. It follows that, when people believe we are saved by "faith only" without obeying God, not only do they have a problem with obedience, but their faith is lacking.

Baptism

Mark 16:15,16 – Jesus sent the apostles to preach the gospel to all the world. He who believes and is baptized will be saved. He who does not believe will be condemned. He who believes what? The message the inspired men preached: the gospel! But what does the gospel say? It says we must believe and be baptized to be saved! People who do not believe baptism is necessary to salvation do not believe the gospel!

Galatians 3:26,27 – We are children of God by **faith**, for as many as were **baptized** into Christ have put Him on. When people have a proper faith, they believe that we come into Christ by baptism. Those who do not believe that, are not children of God by faith.

When people do not believe baptism is necessary to salvation, they have a problem, not just with baptism, but with their faith.

(Colossians 2:12,13)

The church

Acts 8:12 – Those who were baptized believed what Philip preached. He preached, not just about Jesus, but also about the kingdom (church).

Ephesians 5:22-25 – The gospel (which we must believe) teaches that Jesus is the Savior of His body, which is the church.

Many people believe that the church has nothing to do with salvation and it does not matter what church you attend. So they say we should not teach about the church to people who are lost. But people who believe these things do not believe what inspired prophets taught lost sinners about the church. Such people have a problem, not just with the church, but with their faith.

Worship and marriage

1 Timothy 4:1-3 – Some depart from the **faith** forbidding marriage and foods; but people who know and **believe** the truth know better.

Proper faith is not just about who Jesus is. Improper beliefs about worship and about marriage can cause us to depart from the faith.

(James 1:6; 1 Timothy 6:20,21; 2 Timothy 3:8; Titus 1:13)

Our resurrection and future rewards

1 Corinthians 15:11-19 – When we deny the resurrection of the dead, the consequence is that our **faith** is vain and we are still in sin (verses 14,17). Wrong faith leads to condemnation, even among those who believe in Jesus.

2 Timothy 2:18 – When people taught that the resurrection is already past, they strayed from the truth and overthrew *faith*. Though not about who Jesus is, this false doctrine led to false faith.

Those who do not believe in the resurrection of the dead have an improper faith.

(Hebrews 11:6; Romans 6:8)

Conclusion

Matthew 28:18-20 – God expects the knowledge and faith of Christians to ***grow***. We are not required to know and believe everything before we are baptized. It may take time for people to learn and believe some things.

This study has primarily addressed misconceptions about what faith really requires. People who claim salvation "by faith alone" often deny the need for obedience, baptism, church membership, proper worship, etc. Their ideas are false because they contradict what the Bible says about obedience, baptism, etc. But they are also false because they contradict what the Bible says about faith! Such people need to realize they don't even have a true faith!

The Importance of Obedience

Introduction

Many religious people deny that obedience is essential to eternal life.

Hiscox' *Standard Manual for Baptist Churches,* says: "Baptism is not essential to salvation, ... but it is essential to obedience, since Christ has commanded it" (page 21). This admits baptism is essential to obedience, but denies baptism is essential to salvation. The necessary conclusion is that obedience is not essential to salvation. Consider:

"A small boy asked the preacher, 'Sir, what can I do to be saved?' The preacher replied, 'Son, you're too late.' 'What!' exclaimed the boy, 'too late to be saved?' 'No,' said the preacher, 'too late to do anything. You see, son, Jesus already did it all two thousand years ago." (*Pulpit Helps,* 7/84, via *The Christian Chapel Bulletin,* 1/92)

Sam Morris said: "We take the position that a Christian's sins do not damn his soul. The way a Christian lives, what he says, his character, his conduct, or his attitude toward other people has nothing whatever to do with the salvation of his soul. All the prayers a man can pray, all the Bibles he may read, all the churches he may belong to, all the services he may attend, all the sermons he may practice, and all the debts he may pay, all the ordinances he may observe, all the laws he may keep, all the benevolent acts he may perform, will not make his soul one bit safer. And all the sins he may commit from idolatry to murder, will not make his soul in any more danger." (via *Truth Magazine* 3/22/73, page 3)

The purpose of this lesson is to study the Scriptures to determine whether or not obedience is essential to receive eternal life.

We agree that no man will be saved by living a perfectly sinless life (Romans 3:23). And we agree that our obedience does not earn, merit, or deserve eternal life. So, no man will be saved without grace and faith. But having committed sin, are there things a person must do, in addition to grace and faith, to receive forgiveness of sins?

We agree that the blood of Jesus is the only power that can forgive sins. Once a man has sinned, nothing he could do could ever make up for sin without the blood of Jesus. But the question is whether or not the Bible teaches that certain acts of obedience are included as necessary conditions in order to benefit from the cleansing power of Jesus' blood.

We speak to sincerely help each person know how to be saved and have eternal life. Our approach will be to examine basic requirements that religious people generally agree are necessary to salvation. Then we will attempt to see how these doctrines relate to obedience. Do they prove obedience is not essential to salvation, or do they confirm that it is essential?

Obedience and Accepting Jesus as Lord and Savior

Some people say, "You don't need to **do** anything to be saved. Just accept Jesus as your Lord and Savior." But is it really possible to accept Jesus as Lord and Savior without obeying Him?

What Does It Mean to Accept Jesus as Lord?

"Lord" means ruler, master, one who exercises authority. So to "accept Him as Lord" means to obey His rules and submit to His authority.

Luke 6:46 – "But why do you call me 'Lord, Lord,' and do not **do** the things which I say?" Your master is the one you obey (compare Romans 6:16; Matthew 6:24). What right does a person have to claim Jesus as his Lord, if he doesn't obey Him?

Matthew 7:21-27 – To enter the kingdom of heaven, it is not enough to call Jesus "Lord, Lord." The preacher we quoted earlier said there is nothing to do to be saved. But Jesus said one must **do** the will of the Father (verse 21). Hearing and **doing** what Jesus says are like building a house on a rock. If you hear and **don't do**, you are building on sand. Note that Jesus is discussing how to enter the kingdom of heaven (verse 21). To enter, you must **do**. Your claim to accept Him as Lord is empty till you **obey**.

Acts 10:35 – To be acceptable to Him, one must fear Him (respect His authority) and work righteousness (obey His authority).

Suppose I tell you that I ran in an Olympic marathon, but then you find out I was lying in bed the whole time! It is impossible. You cannot run a marathon lying in bed, and you cannot accept Jesus as Lord without obeying Him. When a person teaches that people must accept Jesus as Lord to be saved but do not have to obey Jesus, they contradict Jesus Himself.

(Matthew 28:18-20; Luke 12:47,48; 17:9,10; 1 Corinthians 7:19; Colossians 3:23,24; Hebrews 13:20,21; John 8:31)

What Does It Mean to Accept Jesus as Savior?

If Jesus is the Savior, then we must accept salvation on His terms. He is the one who determines **whom** He will save and what must happen in our lives for Him to save us. What does He say about this?

Hebrews 5:9 – Jesus is the author of salvation to all who **obey** Him. To accept His salvation, we must obey Him. If we believe obedience is not necessary, then we have not accepted the Savior according to His terms. His word says that He saves those who obey Him.

Romans 6:17,18 – To be made free from sin and become servants of righteousness, people must **obey** the teaching delivered. **When** are people made free from sin? When they **obey** the teaching. That's what the Savior says. If we wish to accept Jesus as Savior, then we must accept what He says about the conditions of salvation. (Compare verse 16 and 23.)

1 Peter 1:22,23 – You purify your soul and are born again by **obeying** the truth. When people claim that obedience is unnecessary, they often emphasize being "born again." But how is a person "born again"? By **obeying** the truth, the Word of God. The Bible doctrine of the new birth **requires** obedience.

(Romans 6:3,4; Galatians 3:27; 2 Corinthians 5:17)

Acts 22:10,16 – The lost sinner Saul asked, "What shall I do, Lord?" The preacher we quoted earlier would have replied, "It's too late to do anything. Jesus already did it all." But Jesus said to go into the city and "you will be told all things which are **appointed** for you to **do**" (9:6).

The Lord then sent Ananias, who told Saul to "be baptized and wash away your sins" (verse 16). The Savior never said there is nothing to do to be saved. He said sinners **must do something** to be saved.

To be saved, you must accept Jesus as Lord and Savior. But you must accept Him on His terms as revealed in His word. His word says you cannot accept Him without obedience.

When people say obedience is not essential to salvation, then according to Jesus' word those people do not really understand what it means to accept Him. According to Matthew 7:21-27, He will say, "Depart from me..." because they have not done the will of the Father in heaven.

(James 1:21-25; John 15:14; Philippians 2:12,13; Acts 2:40; 1 Timothy 4:16; 2 Peter 2:20-22)

Obedience and Loving Jesus

1 Corinthians 16:22 – If anyone does not love the Lord Jesus Christ, let him be accursed." Some people say, "I don't think it matters ***how*** you serve the Lord or what you ***do*** in His service. All that matters is that you ***love*** Him." But do you really love Jesus if you don't obey Him? Consider:

Love Is a Form of Obedience.

Matthew 22:36-39 – The two greatest commands are to love God and love your neighbor. So, if we believe that love is essential to salvation, then we must believe that obedience to commands is essential to salvation, because love is a command that must be obeyed!

John 13:34; 15:12 – "This is my commandment, that you love one another, even as I have loved you."

So, love is essential to salvation. But love is a command. So love is a command that is essential to salvation. When a person says obedience to commands is not necessary to salvation, unknowingly he is saying that love is not necessary, for love is a command. It is the greatest of all commands.

(John 15:13,14; 1 John 3:22-24; 4:21; 2 John 5; 1 Timothy 1:5; James 2:8)

Love Requires Us to Obey Other Commands.

John 14:15,21-24 – "If ye love me, you will keep my commands." One who doesn't love, doesn't keep His commands (verse 24). Conclusion: The person who says obedience is not essential, is saying (unintentionally) that you can please God and be saved without loving Him!

1 John 5:3; 2 John 6 – "For this is the love of God, that we keep his commandments."

1 John 3:18 – "Let us not love in word, neither with the tongue, but in **deed** and truth."

Love must show itself in our **actions**. We must obey God's commands. If we don't obey, we don't really love. So obedience is essential to love. But love is essential to salvation. Therefore, obedience is essential to salvation. Instead of proving obedience is not required, the Bible doctrine of love proves the opposite: obedience is necessary to salvation.

(1 John 5:2; 2:5; Romans 13:8-10; Revelation 2:4,5; 1 Thessalonians 1:3; John 15:10; Luke 6:27-36)

Obedience and Saving Faith

One must have faith to be saved (Hebrews 11:6; Mark 16:16; John 8:24 etc.). But some claim, "We are saved by faith alone. As long as you believe in Jesus, it doesn't matter whether or not you do these other things." But is this a correct conclusion?

Faith Is a Form of Obedience.

1 John 3:23,24 – God **commands** us to believe in Jesus; we must keep His commands to abide in Him. If we recognize the importance of faith, we must recognize the importance of obedience, since faith itself is a command from God that we must obey.

John 6:28,29 – People asked what **they must do to work** the works of God. Jesus said the work for them to do is to **believe**.

So, faith is essential to salvation. But faith is a command – a work – something required in obedience to God. Therefore, obedience is essential to salvation, for here is another act of obedience that is required for salvation. If someone claims that works of obedience are not necessary, he is (unintentionally) saying that faith is not necessary.

Saving Faith Requires Us to Obey Other Commands.

Galatians 5:6 – What avails in Christ is faith **working** through love.

James 2:14-26 – Regarding the saving of the soul (verse 14), faith without works is dead like a body without a spirit. It is the kind of faith that demons have. Works are necessary to complete faith (make it perfect). Without obedience, faith is dead and incomplete. We are not saved by faith alone. The faith that justifies is the faith that leads to works.

Hebrews 10:39; 11:8,30, etc. – Here are examples of the kind of faith we must have to save our souls. All examples show that men received God's blessing only after their faith led them to obey His commands. Faith that does not obey is faith that cannot save. (See also verses 7,33,4,17,24,25.)

The Bible doctrine of justification by faith is like the doctrine of love in that, instead of proving obedience is not essential, it proves the opposite. It shows that faith will not save until it moves us to obey. Justification by faith includes obedience; it does not exclude it. We are saved by faith when faith has moved us to obey the conditions of salvation. Without that obedience, we do not have a saving faith.

(John 1:12; 7:17; Romans 1:5; 16:26; 2 Thessalonians 1:11; 1 Thessalonians 1:3; Galatians 2:20; 2 Corinthians 5:7; 1 John 2:29; 1 Peter 1:14; Matthew 12:50; Luke 8:21; Acts 5:32 with Romans 8:9)

Obedience, Repentance, and Confession

Most people who study the Bible will agree that repentance and confession are essential to salvation. But what is the connection between repentance, confession, and obedience?

Repentance Requires Obedience.

Repentance is a Divine command that we must obey to be saved.

Acts 17:30 – God **commands** all men everywhere to repent. So, repentance is a command that must be obeyed.

2 Peter 3:9 – All must come to repentance or they will perish (Luke 13:3,5).

Acts 2:37,38; 3:19 – When people asked what they should do (about their sins), Peter taught that everyone must repent in order to receive **remission** of sins., so their sins may be blotted out. (Luke 24:47; Acts 5:31)

2 Corinthians 7:10 – Godly sorrow produces repentance unto **salvation**.

Like love and faith, repentance is a command that must be obeyed in order to be saved. So here is another act of obedience that is necessary to salvation. To say that obedience is not necessary to salvation would be to say that repentance is not necessary to salvation.

Repentance also requires that people must obey other commands.

Matthew 21:28-32 – The son who had disobeyed his father later regretted it ("repented" – KJV, ASV) and **went**. He **did** the will of the father.

Luke 3:8,9; Acts 26:20 – People who repent must bring forth fruits of repentance: works worthy of repentance. Those who do not bear good fruits will be cast into the fire.

Repentance is a decision – a change of mind or a choice – in which a person determines to turn away from sin and start obeying God. Like love and faith, it is itself an act of obedience, but it also necessarily requires that we obey other Divine commands. The person who denies that obedience is necessary to salvation has not truly repented of sins, for one who truly repents will acknowledge that obedience is necessary!

Confession of Christ Requires Obedience.

Confession of Christ is another act of obedience that the gospel says is necessary to salvation.

Romans 10:9,10 – In order to be saved, one must believe in Christ in his heart and must also confess Christ with his mouth. Note that confession is different from faith: faith is in your heart, but confession is an outward act done with the mouth. Yet, confession is "to salvation."

John 12:42,43 – Some rulers believed in Jesus but refused to confess Him, because they loved the praise of men more than the praise of God. Note again that confession differs from faith. These people believed, but they refused to confess Christ. Were they saved?

Luke 6:46; Matthew 7:21 – Confession is an act of obedience that is necessary to be saved, but it is not all that is necessary. Other forms of obedience are necessary in addition to confession.

(Matthew 10:32; 16:15-18; John 1:49; 4:42; 9:35-38; 11:27; 12:42,43; Acts 8:36-38; 1 Timothy 6:12,13; 1 John 4:15)

When people deny that obedience is necessary to salvation, generally they seek to deny the necessity of baptism. But the gospel clearly states that baptism is essential to salvation, just as it does repentance and confession (see Mark 16:15,16; Acts 2:38; 22:16; Romans 6:3,4; Galatians 3:27; 1 Peter 3:21). In particular, confession involves a physical outward obedience just as surely as baptism does. If we understand that repentance and confession are necessary to salvation, why object to the idea that baptism is necessary to salvation?

Obedience and Receiving Eternal Life at the Judgment

Everyone should seek to receive eternal life at the Judgment. Yet, note the connection to obedience.

We Will Be Judged on the Basis of Our Deeds, Works, and Obedience.

Romans 2:6-10 – God renders to each according to his **works** (verse 6). Those who continue patiently in **doing good** will receive eternal life (verse 7). Those who do not **obey** the truth but **obey** unrighteousness and **work evil**, will receive tribulation and anguish (verses 8,9). But glory and honor await all who **work good** (verse 10). The things we **do** determine our eternal reward.

2 Corinthians 5:10 – Before the judgment-seat of Christ, "each one may receive the things done in the body, according to what he has **done**, whether it be good or bad."

Revelation 20:12,13; 22:12 – Every man will be judged according to his **works**.

Challenge: Can you think of any passage that says we will be judged on the basis of our faith or love at the Judgment? For every one you find (if any) there will be 2 or 3 others that say we will be judged on the basis of **works, deeds, or actions**. Why is this? It is not because faith and love do not matter, but because "works" include faith and love, and because "obedience" is the test of our faith and love.

(John 14:15; James 2:18; Matthew 25:31-46; Acts 17:30,31; John 5:28,29; 1 Peter 4:17,18; Matthew 16:27; 24:46-51; James 2:12; Matthew 25:21ff; 1 Peter 1:17; Revelation 2:23,26; 3:15).

Eternal Life Is for Those Who Obey God.

John 5:28,29 – All people are raised to life or condemnation depending on whether they **did good or did evil**.

1 John 2:17 – "He that **does the will of God** abides forever."

2 Thessalonians 1:8,9 – Those who **obey not the gospel** will receive vengeance in flaming fire. They are punished with everlasting destruction from the presence of the Lord.

Romans 2:7 – Eternal life is for those who are patient in **doing good**.

Note it carefully: Men say that what you **do** has nothing to do with your eternal destiny. The gospel says that **what we do is the very basis on which our eternal destinies will be determined.** Go figure! How can any two beliefs be more contradictory?

(Luke 10:25,28,37; John 6:27; Romans 8:12,13; 1 Timothy 6:17-19; Galatians 6:8-10; Matthew 12:50; James 4:17 with Romans 6:23; Galatians 5:19-21; John 12:50; 2 Peter 1:10,11; Hebrews 10:36; Ephesians 2:2; 5:6; Colossians 3:6; 2 Corinthians 10:5,6; Hebrews 2:2ff; Philippians 2:12,13; Revelation 14:13).

Conclusion

Consider the consequences of what we have learned about obedience.

The gospel teaches that:

* If I want to truly accept Jesus as Lord and Savior, then I must obey Him.

* If I want to truly love God, then I must obey Him.

* If I want to have a true saving faith in Jesus, then I must obey Him.

* In order to truly repent of sins and confess Christ, then I must obey Him.
* If I want to stand justified and receive eternal life in the Judgment Day, then I must obey Him.

So, obedience is essential to salvation. We must be "doers of the word."

1 John 2:3-6 – To know Him and abide in Him, we must **keep his commands, keep his word**. If we are not doing so, but still claim to know Him, we are liars, and we don't abide in Him. (Remember what happens to liars – Revelation 21:8; John 15:5,6.)

1 John 3:6-8,10 – If we want to be righteous, we must **practice** righteousness. If we practice sin, we are of the Devil. If we don't practice righteousness, we are not of God. (Compare 3:24.)

Have you obeyed the Lord in receiving forgiveness of sin? Are you living a faithful life?

Godly Sorrow or Worldly Sorrow?

2 Corinthians 7:10 – Godly sorrow produces repentance leading to salvation, not to be regretted; but the sorrow of the world produces death.

In order to be forgiven of sins, one must first repent. In order to repent, one must first have godly sorrow. Some people do not repent because they are not really sorry. But there is another kind of sorrow – the sorrow of the world – that does not lead to repentance, but leads to death.

If godly sorrow is necessary in order to repent and receive salvation, but there is another kind of sorrow that leads to death, then surely we need to know the difference.

What is the difference between godly sorrow and worldly sorrow? How do we recognize when we or others have a proper sorrow for our sins?

Consider the Bible teaching:

The Need for Godly Sorrow and Repentance

Passages about the Necessity of Repentance

God's word places far more emphasis on repentance than many of us appreciate.

Mark 1:15 – Mark summarized Jesus' message as: "Repent, and believe in the gospel."

Luke 24:47 – Jesus said repentance and remission of sin should be taught to all nations.

Acts 2:38 – In the first gospel sermon, Peter preached, "Repent and be baptized, every one of you for the remission of sins..."

Acts 17:30 – God commands all men everywhere to repent.

2 Peter 3:9 – God is not willing for men to perish but wants all to come to repentance.

Acts 8:22 – Christians who sin must be taught to repent of their wickedness.

Revelation 3:19 – As many as I love, I rebuke and chasten. Therefore be zealous and repent.

Repentance is a **change of mind** – a decision, a choice, a deliberate exercise of the will – in which one determines to act differently in the future than he has in the past. If you have sinned, you must admit the sin and be sorry. Then you must make up your mind to **change**.

Forgiveness comes only after a decision to change! Without repentance no one can be saved.

(Matthew 3:2; 11:20-24; 21:28-32; Luke 13:3; Ezekiel 18:21-23,27,28,30-32; 33:10-19; 2 Timothy 2:25,26; Romans 2:4,5; Acts 3:19; 8:22; 5:31; Revelation 2:5,16,21-23; Luke 3:8,9; 15:7,10; 17:3,4; 2 Corinthians 12:21; 1 Kings 8:46-50; 2 Chronicles 6:24-29; 7:14; Joel 2:12-14; Jeremiah 36:3,7; Isaiah 55:7)

Passages about the Necessity of Godly Sorrow

True repentance must be motivated by acknowledgement of error and sincere sorrow or remorse for sin.

Proverbs 28:13 – One who covers his sins will not prosper. In order to have mercy, he must confess and forsake sin.

Joel 2:12,13 – Turn to God with weeping and mourning. Tear your heart, not your garment.

Luke 18:13 – The publican, seeking forgiveness for his sins, beat his breast saying, "God be merciful to me, a sinner."

James 4:8-10 – Sinners must mourn and weep.

2 Corinthians 7:10 – Godly sorrow produces repentance leading to salvation...

Before one will change his life, he must **decide** to change (repent). Before he decides to change, he must recognize that he has been guilty. Then he must sincerely regret what he did and sincerely wish he had never done it.

A person will never truly repent until he knows and admits he was wrong and is truly sorry. Do you recognize your sins? Are you truly sorry?

(Psalm 38:18; 34:18; 51:17; 31:10; Isaiah 57:15; 66:2; 22:12-14; Job 42:6; Jeremiah 31:19; 5:3; 6:26; Jonah 3:5-8; Matthew 26:75; 11:20; 2 Chronicles 34:27; Ezra 10:1; (1 John 1:9; 1 Kings 8:47; 2 Chron. 6:24-39; 7:14; Acts 19:18; James 5:16;

Jeremiah 3:12,13; 8:4-6; 5:3; 44:4,5; Jonah 3:8,10; Amos 4:6-11; Luke 15:18,21; 17:3,4; Psalm 32:5; Lev. 26:40)

Godly Sorrow vs. Worldly Sorrow

A person may cease a sinful practice without repenting. A person may admit an act was wrong without being sorry. But a person may be sorry yet still not forgiven because it is improper sorrow. So let us consider the difference between godly sorrow and worldly sorrow.

Examples of Godly Sorrow

Godly sorrow requires true remorse, sincere acknowledgment of error, and determination not repeat the sin. We must grieve for the harm done to our relationship to God and other people, truly wishing we never had done it.

Consider Bible examples:

David

2 Samuel 12:9-14 – The prophet Nathan convicted David of adultery with Bathsheeba and having her husband killed. David confessed that he had sinned, so God forgave him. But he would still suffer consequences: the sword would never depart from his house, he would have opposition within his own family, and the child who had been conceived would die.

This account does not describe his sorrow, but David describes it in the book of Psalms.

Psalm 32:1-5 – "Blessed is he whose transgression is forgiven, whose sin is covered..." David describes his groaning, grief, and agony while he remained in sin. Forgiveness required that he acknowledge his sin, not hide it. He must confess it to the Lord without deceit (sincerely).

Psalm 38:18 – I will declare my iniquity and be in anguish for my sin. Forgiveness required admitting the sin with anguish because he had done it. Notice the depth of sorrow.

Psalm 51:1-4,7-10 – David pled for mercy from God to cleanse his transgressions and sins. He acknowledged his sin, constantly aware of his guilt. He grieved especially for the wrong he had done against God.

2 Samuel 15:26 (16:11) – When he fled because Absalom rebelled, David said, "Let Him do to me as seems good to Him."

This is godly sorrow. One must openly acknowledge his sin and truly grieve for the wrongs he has done, sincerely wishing he had never committed them. David suffered severe consequences in this life without rebelling against them, but what grieved him most was what his sin did to his relationship to God and his need for cleansing of the burden of guilt.

Ninevites

Matthew 12:41 – Jesus said the people of Nineveh repented at the preaching of Jonah.

Jonah 3:4-10 describes this repentance. From the king down, the people believed the message from God, wore sackcloth and fasted (signs of grief), and cried to God. Everyone was required to turn from his evil way and from the violence in his hand.

The people sincerely grieved for their sins and determined to change their conduct (repent). Then they prayed to God for forgiveness. Godly sorrow led to repentance unto forgiveness.

The prodigal son – Luke 15

Verses 11-16 – The son wasted his father's inheritance in sin (with harlots – verse 30). When the money was gone, he ended up feeding hogs and would have eaten the hog slop.

Note verse 16 – No one gave him anything. The account shows that his father knew what was happening but did not bail his son out. He would have let him eat hog slop as the consequence of his sins.

Far too often parents or friends bail out a sinner to help him avoid the consequences of his sins. If instead they allow him to suffer the consequences of his sins, he may be led to repent like the prodigal did. (2 Thessalonians 3:10)

Verses 17-19 – As a result, the son came to himself. He decided to go home and admit that he had sinned against heaven and against his father. And he offered to accept whatever consequences followed: he no longer deserved to be a son, but was willing to be demoted to a servant.

A person who has godly sorrow just wants to make his life right with God and with people whom he has wronged. This requires admitting his sins, pleading for forgiveness, changing his life, and accepting whatever consequences follow. His main concern is being forgiven of his guilt.

(Peter – Matthew 26:75; Paul – 1 Timothy 1:12-16)

Examples of Worldly Sorrow

Worldly sorrow is more concerned with avoiding the consequences of the sin in this life than with changing the conduct or with correcting the relationship with God and those who have been wronged. Consider Bible examples:

Cain – Genesis 4

Verses 1-7 – Abel's sacrifice pleased God, whereas Cain's did not. Cain responded, not with repentance, but with anger (verse 5). God told Cain not to be angry but to rule over the sin.

Verses 8-12 – Cain killed Abel then denied responsibility and lied to God, saying he did not know where Abel was. God said he would be punished because the ground would no longer produce for him, and he would be a vagabond on the earth.

Verses 13,14 – Cain complained that his punishment was greater than he could bear.

Contrast this to the examples of godly sorrow. When his worship was not accepted, he became angry. When rebuked for the anger, he killed Abel. When questioned about that, he lied to God. When told he would be punished, he sought to avoid punishment. At no point did Cain acknowledge sin or ask forgiveness. Instead of repenting, he just went deeper and deeper into sin.

King of Israel – 2 Kings 6:24-33

Verses 25-29 – The northern kingdom of Israel was ruled by a son of wicked king Ahab. As punishment for their sins, the nation was besieged by Syria. This caused a famine so severe that women were actually eating their own children.

Verse 30 – The king responded with grief in which he wore sackcloth and tore his clothes.

Verses 31 – Rather than repenting, the king determined to behead the prophet Elisha.

The king knew the distress occurred because the nation was alienated from God. But rather than seeking forgiveness to restore their relationship with God, instead he sought to slay God's prophet. Rather than repenting, he fought against the consequences of the sin.

King Saul – 1 Samuel

At first Saul was humble but he changed.

He sought to please the people rather than to please God.

13:13,14 – Instead of waiting for Samuel, Saul himself offered sacrifice to God. Samuel said he had disobeyed God's command and as a result his dynasty would not continue.

15:13-15,20-23 – God told Saul and Israel to kill all the Amalekites and destroy their flocks. Instead they spared the king and the best of the flocks and herds. Saul said he had obeyed God. Then he blamed the people for keeping the best animals to the offer the sacrifices. Samuel said rebellion and stubbornness are like witchcraft and idolatry. So God rejected Saul from being king.

15:24,25,30 – Saul admitted he had sinned because he feared the people, but still wanted to be honored before the people. He was concerned, not about God's forgiveness, but about what the people thought.

God chose David to replace Saul.

Throughout Saul's remaining life he struggled to defeat the consequences of sin.

16:23; 18:8-12 – Saul's jealousy led him to try to kill David who played music to calm him.

19:4-6,9,11-17 – Saul swore to his son Jonathan not to kill David. But then he tried again to kill him with his spear. Then he sent messengers to kill David in his bed.

20:30-33 – Saul told Jonathan to help kill David so Jonathan could become king. When Jonathan objected, Saul tried to kill Jonathan.

22:11-19 – Saul killed all the priests and their families because he claimed they helped David.

24:16-20; 26:21-25 – Twice David could have killed Saul but spared him. Both times Saul admitted he had sinned. He wept and admitted David was more righteous than he was. He promised to no longer harm David. But both times immediately he continued trying to kill him.

28:15-20 – When God refused to give Saul guidance, he used a medium to call up Samuel.

1 Chronicles 10:13 – Saul died for his unfaithfulness which he had committed against the LORD, because he did not keep the word of the LORD, and also because he consulted a medium...

Saul's attitude was back and forth, back and forth. He admitted sin, vowed to do right, and grieved for his circumstances, but he immediately returned to sin. He was more concerned about pleasing the people and avoiding the consequences of his sins than he was about pleasing God and seeking God's forgiveness.

People today would doubtless say he was mentally ill. But God held him accountable and continued to bring consequences and punishment for his sin.

(Israel – Numbers 13,14; Rich young ruler)

Applications

Many people today are not forgiven because they never have godly sorrow for their sins.

Godly sorrow leads one to grieve for his sin, its effect on his relationship to God and harm done to others. It leads to humble acknowledging of sin and sincere repentance: a decision to change so one can please God.

With godly sorrow, the sinner acknowledges his guilt and seeks above all else to change so he can be forgiven and be right with God.

2 Corinthians 7:10 – "Godly sorrow works repentance unto salvation."

Psalm 38:18 – "I will declare my iniquity and be in anguish for my sin."

Psalm 51:3,4 – "I acknowledge my transgressions, and my sin is always before me. Against You, You only, have I sinned, and done this evil in Your sight..."

Proverbs 28:13 – He who covers his sins will not prosper, but whoever confesses and forsakes them will have mercy.

With godly sorrow, the sinner focuses on his need for forgiveness, cleansing of guilt and restoration of his relationship with God and others. He accepts consequences in this life if only God will forgive him.

David said: "Blessed is he whose transgression is forgiven, whose sin is covered..."

The prodigal said: "Father, I have sinned against heaven and in thy sight. I am no more worthy to be called thy son. Make me as one of your hired servants."

Godly sorrow leads a person to deeply regret the harm done to his relationship to God and other people. He openly admits his sin, willingly apologizes, accepts consequences in this life, and seeks forgiveness according to whatever terms God requires.

Godly sorrow focuses on the need to change and be forgiven.

Worldly sorrow often leads, not to change, but to excuses or committing more sins. The sinner feels sorry for himself and regrets the consequences in this life and the fact he did not get his way.

With worldly sorrow, the sinner may seek to hide his guilt. If his sin is exposed, instead of changing, he may become angry or go deeper into sin.

When rebuked for his worship, Cain became angry, killed Abel, and then lied to God.

Saul first said he had obeyed God. Then he blamed the people. Then he spent the rest of his life trying to kill the man appointed to take his place as king.

Worldly sorrow may lead the sinner to deny sin, blame others, or rationalize. It often leads to other sins. In any case, it does not lead to a sincere effort to change.

With worldly sorrow one may focus on avoiding the consequences in this life.

Cain: "My punishment is greater than I can bear."

Saul: "I have sinned, yet honor me before the people."

Criminals may sorrow, not for the crime, but for the fact they got caught and punished.

Sexually immoral people may regret having a disease, unwanted pregnancy, or divorce.

Drunkards, drug abusers, or gamblers may regret loss of finances, jobs, or family.

People guilty of other scandals may regret exposure, loss of power, influence, or position.

With worldly sorrow, the sinner focuses on himself and avoiding consequences.

Conclusion

Godly sorrow and repentance are not the same thing, but godly sorrow leads to repentance. And both are necessary to salvation. No one will be saved simply because he is sorry, if he does not decide to repent. And no one who changes his conduct will be saved unless he is truly sorry for what he did.

Forgiveness of sins requires:

Recognizing and admitting our conduct was sinful

Sincere godly sorrow that we have wronged God and others

Repentance with a sincere determination to change

Asking for forgiveness. For one who was never forgiven by God, this is done in baptism. For an erring child of God this is done by confession in prayer and apology to people wronged.

Change of conduct: quit practicing sin and make restitution

Have you and I been truly sorry for our sins so we have repented and received forgiveness?

(Matthew 5:23,24; Luke 17:3,4; James 5:16; Ezekiel 18:21-32; 33:14,15; Proverbs 28:13; Acts 26:20; Luke 3:8-14; Matthew 3:8; Matthew 21:28-31; Exodus 22:1-15; Leviticus 6:1-5; Numbers 5:5-8; 2 Samuel 12:6)

Repentance

Introduction:

One of the most common themes of faithful teachers throughout the Scriptures is the need for repentance.

Consider just a few examples:

Old Testament prophets

Jeremiah 25:4,5 – Repent now everyone of his evil way and his evil doing... This was a typical message of the Old Testament prophets. They repeatedly preached the need for repentance (often expressing the concept by using terms such as "turn" or "return.")

(Jeremiah 35:15; Ezekiel 18:30; 2 Kings 17:13)

John the Baptist

Matthew 3:2 – John the Baptist taught, "Repent, for the kingdom of heaven is at hand!"

Jesus

Mark 1:15 – Mark summarized Jesus' message as: "Repent, and believe in the gospel."

Luke 13:3 – Unless you repent you will all likewise perish.

Revelation 3:19 – As many as I love, I rebuke and chasten. Therefore be zealous and repent.

Apostles and prophets of the early church

Acts 2:38 – In the first gospel sermon, Peter preached, "Repent and be baptized, every one of you for the remission of sins..."

Acts 17:30 – God commands all men everywhere to repent.

All who study the Bible agree that repentance is fundamental to Bible teaching.

(Mark 6:12)

The purpose of this lesson is to study what the Bible says about repentance.

Despite the frequent Bible references, many people misunderstand repentance and many more neglect it. Even though they may be guilty of immorality, indifference, mistreatment of others, or doctrinal error, many people never truly repent. Note that people who are not Christians need to repent, but so do Christians when we sin. This is a lesson needed by everyone.

What is repentance and why is it important?

The Meaning of Repentance

A Change of Mind

The basic message of the gospel is **change**. To be forgiven of sins, you must **change**. To please God you must **change**. To receive eternal life you must **change**. This emphasis on change is focused in the word "repent."

> "Repentance" (μετανοια) – "a change of mind: as it appears in one who repents of a purpose he has formed or of something he has done ... esp. the change of mind of those who have begun to abhor their errors and misdeeds, and have determined to enter upon a better course of life..." – Grimm-Wilke-Thayer.

Repentance is "a **change of mind**" – a decision, a choice, a deliberate exercise of the will – in which one determines to act differently in the future than he has in the past.

Examples of Repentance

Jonah 3:4-10 – When Jonah preached, the people of Nineveh gave heed, were sorry, and turned from their evil ways (verses 8,10). Jesus said these people "repented" at Jonah's preaching (Matthew 12:41).

Matthew 21:28-32 – A son refused to work for his father, but later repented (regretted it – NKJV) and went. He "changed his mind." Jesus applied this to sinners who repented at John's preaching in contrast to priests would not.

Repentance from Sin

Specifically, the gospel requires men to repent or change their minds about **sin**. This involves making up one's mind to cease practicing sin and to become obedient to God.

Luke 24:47 – Those who are not God's children should be taught the need for repentance and remission of *sin*. That for which men need remission is *sin*!

Acts 8:22 – Likewise, Christians who sin need to be taught to repent of their wickedness. (Luke 15:7,10; 17:3,4; 2 Corinthians 12:21)

Repentance is a decision to cease sinning and begin serving God instead.

(2 Timothy 2:25,26; Matthew 9:13; Ezekiel 14:6; Deuteronomy 30:2,8,10; Jeremiah 8:4-6; 3:7,10-14; 25:3-7; 36:3,7; 2 Kings 17:13; Zechariah 1:3,4; 2 Chronicles 30:6-9; 1 Samuel 7:3,4; Revelation 2:5)

Things That Must Precede Repentance

Before people can truly repent, certain other things must occur. Sometimes people fail to properly repent because they misunderstand or fail to practice the things that must precede it.

One Must Hear and Believe God's Will.

Learning and believing are necessary in order to inform men that they need to repent and to motivate them to do so.

Teaching is necessary to lead one to repent. Remember that Jesus, the prophets, and the apostles all **preached and taught** repentance.

Luke 24:47 – Jesus commanded that repentance and remission should be **preached** to all men. Men cannot know they need to repent unless they are told to repent.

2 Kings 17:13 – God repeatedly sent prophets to warn the people to repent. Every Old Testament prophet you can name preached this way. Today people sometimes tire of hearing preachers rebuke sin. But read the prophets! This is God's plan. His way to lead men to leave sin is to warn them to repent.

2 Timothy 2:25,26 – We should correct those who are in error hoping they will come to repentance and escape the snare of the devil. No one will ever change until he realizes he is wrong and sees the consequence of his error. To convince people they are wrong we must show them what God's word says.

Romans 2:4,5 – Failure to repent treasures up wrath at the day of judgment. It is not unkind or cruel to tell people in sin that they need to repent. It is an act of love, because only in this way can they correct their lives and receive eternal life.

The message that leads men to repent must be God's word.

Ezekiel 13:22 – People continued in sin when false prophets failed to tell them they needed to turn (repent) from their wicked ways. When people sin, faithful preachers must not let them continue thinking they are acceptable before God. If we do not rebuke them, they may be lost.

Ezekiel 33:7-9,14-16 – If people are lost because preachers did not warn them of their sins, God will also hold the preachers accountable. Some people cannot bring themselves to tell folks they are wrong. God will hold such teachers accountable for the lost souls that result.

People in sin need to hear exactly what God's word says. Withholding the truth does no one a favor.

(Jeremiah 23:12; 26:2,3; Isaiah 6:10; 2 Corinthians 7:8ff; Acts 20:21; 17:30; 26:20; Luke 16:27-31; 5:32; Jonah 3:4,5; Proverbs 1:23; Revelation 3:19)

One Must Acknowledge Sin.

Hearing the truth leads honest people to be convicted of their sins.

Psalm 38:18 – I will declare my iniquity.

Proverbs 28:13 – One who covers his sin will not prosper. In order to have mercy, he must confess and forsake it.

Malachi 3:7 – When confronted about their sins, some people refuse to admit guilt. They ask, "What sin? What do I have to repent of?"

Before one will change his life, he must **decide** to change (repent). Before he decides to change, he must recognize that he has been guilty. As long as a person defends or justifies his practice and refuses to admit error, he has not repented.

(1 John 1:9; 1 Kings 8:47; 2 Chronicles 6:24-39; 7:14; Acts 19:18; James 5:16; Jeremiah 3:12f; 8:4-6; 5:3; 44:4,5; Jonah 3:8,10; Amos 4:6-11; Luke 15:18,21; 17:3,4; Psalm 32:5; Leviticus 26:40)

One Must Be Sorry for His Sins.

Simply admitting one has sinned is not enough. Some people know they have sinned but they don't care, or at least don't really regret what they did.

Psalm 38:18 – I will declare my iniquity and be in anguish for my sin.

Joel 2:12,13 – Turn to God (repent) with weeping and mourning. Tear your heart, not your garment. God wants, not mere outward expressions of grief, but sincere sorrow. We must sincerely wish we had never done the act.

2 Corinthians 7:10 – Godly sorrow leads to repentance unto salvation. One who does not repent cannot be saved, but he cannot truly repent without sorrow.

People sometimes observe that a man has stopped committing a sin, so they say, "He must have repented." But a person may admit he did wrong and may even stop committing the sin, but that does not prove he regrets what he did. He may think it was justified under the circumstances.

People who are caught and convicted of a crime may admit they were guilty, but that does not mean they are sorry for the crime. They may be sorry only for the fact they got caught.

A couple who live together without marriage may get married; they are no longer committing fornication, but that does not prove they regret the fornication they committed.

To be saved one must Scripturally repent. But He will never truly repent until he knows he was wrong, admits he was wrong, and is truly sorry. Do you recognize your sins and are you truly sorry?

(James 4:8,9; Psalm 34:18; 51:17; 31:10; Isaiah 57:15; 66:2; 22:12-14; Job 42:6; Jeremiah 31:19; 5:3; 6:26; Jonah 3:5-8; Matthew 26:75; 11:20; 2 Chronicles 34:27; Ezra 10:1)

The Importance of Repentance

Frequently I have heard people say that repentance means "being sorry." So they think if they just admit they were wrong and say they are sorry, everything is forgiven. But repentance is more than that. Repentance is a decision to ***change***. Why is this important?

Repentance Is Essential in Order to Develop Proper Attitudes.

We can never please God till we develop a proper state of mind.

Proverbs 4:23 – Keep your heart diligently because out of it are the issues of life. The mind is where we decide what we will do. People do wrong because they ***chose*** to do wrong. In order to start doing right, they must change their mind and decide to do right: repent!

Romans 6:17,18 – One who is a servant of sin needs to be made free from sin and become a servant of righteousness. To do this, he must obey God "from the heart." A person cannot obey from the heart until he has decided in his heart to obey.

We can never please God till we get our heart right. That happens in repentance. When people know what God wants but will not do it, they lack repentance. (They may also lack faith, love, etc., but one thing they definitely lack is repentance.)

(Joel 2:12,13; 1 Kings 8:33-36,46-50; 2 Chronicles 6:24-39; 7:14; Ezekiel 18:31; Jeremiah 24:7; 2 Kings 23:25; 1 Samuel 7:3,4)

Repentance Is Essential in order to Receive God's Forgiveness.

2 Peter 3:9 – God is not willing for men to perish but wants all to come to repentance. The alternative to repentance is perishing! (Luke 13:3,5)

Ezekiel 18:21-23,27,28,30-32 – Wicked men must turn from evil and do right or they will die (spiritually). God does not want us to die. He is willing to forgive, but first we must be willing to **change**. Before we can change, we must **decide** to change – that is repentance.

The gospel emphasizes repentance because repentance is essential to changing our attitudes and our lives. Until we are willing to change our lives, God is not willing to forgive our sins!

If you have sinned, you must admit the sin and be sorry. Then you must make up your mind to **change**. Have you done so, or are you just expecting everything to be forgotten because you said you were sorry? Forgiveness comes only after a decision to change!

(Acts 2:38; Ezekiel 33:10-19; 2 Timothy 2:25,26; Romans 2:4,5; Acts 3:19; 8:22; 5:31; 17:30,31; Revelation 2:5,16,21-23; Luke 3:8,9; 24:47; 2 Corinthians 7:10; 1 Kings 8:46-50; 2 Chronicles 6:24-29; 7:14; Joel 2:12-14; Jeremiah 36:3,7; Isaiah 55:7; Matthew 11:20-24; 21:28-32)

Things That Must Follow Repentance

The decision to change constitutes repentance, but something more must follow the repentance.

After Repentance, One Must Meet Other Conditions of Forgiveness.

What the conditions are depends on whether one has already become a child of God.

One who is not a child of God must repent and be baptized.

Acts 2:38 – Repent and be **baptized** for remission of sins. Some people do not realize that the Bible teaches baptism is essential. Other people have been taught this but refuse to accept it. Remember, repentance is a decision to obey God's word. When a person sees that God's word requires baptism to be saved, if he has truly repented he will gladly obey.

Some Christians fail to adequately emphasize repentance in teaching alien sinners. Instead they put the primary emphasis on baptism. But baptism does no good if one has not truly repented.

When a person refuses to be baptized, his primary problem is not baptism: his problem is a lack of true faith or a lack of repentance! When he **believes** the **truth**, he will realize that he must repent and be baptized. If he then truly **repents**, you won't be able to keep him from the water!

(Mark 16:15,16; Acts 2:38; 22:16; Romans 6:3,4; Galatians 3:27; 1 Peter 3:21)

A child of God who sins must repent and pray for forgiveness.

Sometimes children of God sin after they have been baptized. They do not need to be baptized again, but they do need to repent again and then confess their sins.

Acts 8:22 – Simon was told to repent and pray that his sin might be forgiven. The Christian who sins needs to repent and pray, not repent and be baptized. (1 John 1:9; Matthew 6:12)

Matthew 5:23,24 – If one has wronged other people, he must also confess to them. If the sin is known and has been a bad influence on the congregation or hindered the effort of the church to teach, then the whole church needs to be told the person has repented.

Sometimes a member says he must "go before the church and repent." This is inaccurate. Repentance is done in the heart. If you have not already repented before you come forward, there is no point in coming forward. The reason to come forward is, not to repent, but to **confess** and to ask for prayers (Acts 8:24; James 5:16).

(Luke 17:3,4; 15:18,21; Genesis 50:17; James 5:16; Proverbs 28:13; study passages on influence and reputation)

Then One Must Change His Conduct: Quit Practicing Sin.

Repentance is a **decision** to change. After receiving forgiveness, one must follow through and **make** the changes he decided to make.

Scriptures

Acts 26:20 – Repentance must lead to **works** worthy of repentance. (Luke 3:8-14; Matthew 3:8)

Ezekiel 18:21-32 – To avoid death, the wicked must turn from evil, **do** right, and keep God's statutes.

Proverbs 28:13 – To prosper, we must not hide our sins, but confess and *forsake* them.

(Matthew 21:28-31)

Applications

This is where many people fail. They want forgiveness, so they are baptized or pray for forgiveness; but they never follow through and **change**. They want forgiveness but not **change**.

There is a difference between repentance and the **fruits** of repentance. Sometimes people go through the motions of baptism (or public confession), but do not truly repent. These people will never be forgiven until they first truly repent.

Other people really do repent and intend to change their lives, but they never follow through and change their lives. These people may have been forgiven when they repented, but now they are back in sin. They need to repent again and then produce the fruits of repentance.

(Genesis 44 compare Genesis 37; Luke 13:5-9; 15:19; Ezekiel 33:10-19; Revelation 2:5; Deuteronomy 30:2; 2 Kings 17:13; Jonah 3:8,10; Isaiah 55:7; Jeremiah 4:1; 18:8,11; 44:4,5; 25:3-7; 35:15; 2 Chronicles 30:6-9; 1 Samuel 7:3,4)

Then One Must Make Restitution.

Repentance requires more than just deciding to do right "next time" or to "never do that again." To the extent possible we must attempt to correct the harmful effects of our sins on other people.

Ezekiel 33:14,15 – When one was been wicked, he must not only walk in the statutes, but must also return what he stole. (Exodus 22:1-15; Leviticus 6:1-5; Numbers 5:5-8; 2 Samuel 12:6)

Luke 19:8 – Zacchaeus had been a tax collector. When he was converted, he determined to return the taxes he had charged wrongfully.

Ezra 10:3,11,17,19,44 – When Israelite men violated God's law by marrying foreign women, repentance required them to put away those wives. Repentance requires the same thing today when people are living in adultery because of unscriptural divorce and remarriage. (9:1-10:44; Matthew 19:9)

This can be a difficult principle to apply because sometimes the effect of a sin cannot be undone (for example, murder). But it is a Bible principle and must be accomplished to the extent possible.

(Philem. 10-14,18,19; Matthew 21:28-31; Nehemiah 5:11-13; 2 Corinthians 7:9-11; Genesis 20:1-14; 1 Samuel 12:3; Proverbs 6:31; Acts 16:33; 26:20; 19:18,19)

Conclusion

Luke 15:17-24 – The prodigal son illustrates all the principles we have studied. The younger son wasted his inheritance in riotous living (verses 13,30). When he "came to himself" he determined to return (verses 14-17). Notice the elements of repentance and forgiveness. (The story does not use the word "repent," but the parallel stories do in verses 7,10.)

* He **acknowledged his error**: "I have sinned" (verse 18).

* His **sorrow** was implied by the fact he no longer thought he was worthy to be a son (verse 19).

* He then **decided** to go back to the father (verses 18,19). This is repentance. (Compare verses 7,10.)

* He met the conditions of forgiveness by **confessing** his sin to the father (verses 20,21).

* He **changed his conduct**: he left the practice of sin (verses 20,21).

* He offered to make **restitution** by being just a servant of the father (verses 19,21).

When the son did return the father rejoiced (verses 20,22-24). Truly there is joy in heaven among the angels when a sinner "repents" (verses 7,10).

The gospel is a message of **change**. Sinners can change. You can change. Do you need to repent and be baptized? Are you a child of God who needs to repent and confess error and ask for the prayers of the church?

Confession of Christ

Introduction:

When they think about "confession," most people think about admitting guilt, which is unpleasant. But we can also confess good things. For example, we may confess that we love our husband or wife, our children, our country, etc. Occasionally one sees an announcement in a paper or a billboard where a man says: "Joan, I love you. Bill." That is a confession.

To confess means to declare, acknowledge, profess, or admit.

One confesses when he openly declares that he is convinced a thing is true. Confession is the opposite of denial or silence. Three elements are needed for a proper confession:

(1) A ***belief*** in the heart that a certain thing is true.

(2) A ***decision*** that one is ***willing*** to make an open commitment and let others know.

(3) A ***statement*** acknowledging, professing, or declaring the conviction.

The purpose of this lesson is to study confession that is necessary in conversion.

We will consider what it means to confess Christ and learn what role confession has in becoming a Christian or being saved from sin.

The Bible mentions many things that can be confessed, including confessing sins. But this study discusses primarily confession of Christ. Confession of Christ should continue after conversion, but we will emphasize confessing Christ as part of conversion.

What Is Confession of Christ?

Some Confessions that Are NOT Confession of Christ

"God for Christ's sake has forgiven my sin."

Some religious groups expect people to make such a confession before baptism.

One group asks people before baptism: "...have you accepted Jesus Christ as your personal Savior, and do you believe that God, for Christ's sake, has forgiven your sins, and given you a new heart?" (Seventh Day Adventist "Baptismal Vow," via *Handbook of Religious Quotations*).

Other groups require a person to tell an experience from his life that proves he has been saved or born again before they will baptize him.

Yet no Bible passage anywhere teaches anyone to make such a confession or tell such an experience in order to be baptized.

The reason is simple: sins are ***not*** forgiven before baptism.

Acts 22:16 – Be baptized and wash away your sins.

Acts 2:38 – Repent and be baptized for remission of sins.

Mark 16:16 – He that believes and is baptized shall be saved.

1 Peter 3:21 – Baptism also now saves us.

For one to confess that he was saved or forgiven or born again ***before*** he was baptized, would be an unscriptural and invalid confession, because it simply is not true.

Confession of Sin

When a person has committed sin, confessing this is good. In fact, children of God who sin are required to confess sin to be forgiven (1 John 1:9; Matthew 6:12).

But no passage teaches that confession of sins is a required step to conversion. And if people did make such a confession, it would not be sufficient for them to be saved. There is a confession that is required to be forgiven, but it is not a confession of ***sins.***

The same could be said for other confessions people might make regarding salvation, the church, or the Bible. Nothing in the gospel ***requires*** one to confess such things to become a child of God, nor would such confessions be sufficient to meet the gospel requirements in order to be saved.

But there is something that must be confessed so one can be saved. What is it?

What Confession of Christ IS

Matthew 10:32 – Everyone who confesses Jesus before men, Jesus will confess him before the Father. Note that this is a confession about ***Jesus:*** It is a statement about who Jesus is.

Let us consider at this point what it **means** to **confess Christ.** Then later we will show that we **must** confess Christ as part of conversion in order to be forgiven of sins and become a child of God.

Confess Jesus as Christ/King

Matthew 16:15-18 – Jesus asked the disciples who they believed He was (note that prompting others to make a confession is proper to do). Peter said He was the **Christ,** the Son of God. "Christ" means one who is "anointed" to be king, ruler of God's people. Jesus blessed Peter and said that this truth was revealed from the Father.

1 Timothy 6:13; Matthew 27:11 – Jesus witnessed "the good confession" before Pilate. When Pilate asked, "Are you the King of the Jews," Jesus answered, "It is as you say" (NKJV). (Other translations say "Thou sayest" meaning "it is just as thou sayest, to be sure, certainly" – Grimm-Wilke-Thayer.) (Compare Matthew 26:25,64 with Mark 14:62; John 18:33,36,37; Luke 23:3; Mark 14:2.)

"King of the Jews" was an expression for Christ, who descended from David and would be anointed King over Israel. Yet Jesus clearly told Pilate He would not be an earthly king (John 18:36). He confessed Himself to be a **spiritual** King: the Christ. (Compare John 1:49.)

Note that this confession was so important that Jesus was willing to make it knowing that it would lead to His condemnation and death.

So, when people today confess Christ, they must mean that He is the Christ, the anointed King or Ruler over all mankind and especially over God's people.

(Other examples: John 4:25,26;9:22; 11:27; 12:42; Matthew 26:63,64; Acts 8:37; Philippians 2:11)

Confess Jesus as the Son of God

Matthew 3:16,17; 17:5 – The heavenly Father Himself confessed Jesus to be His beloved Son both at Jesus' baptism and at the Transfiguration

Matthew 16:16 – Peter confessed Jesus to be the Christ, the **Son of the Living God.**

John 1:49 – Nathanael confessed, "You are the Son of God! You are the King of Israel!"

John 11:27 – Martha confessed, "I believe that You are the Christ, the Son of God."

John 20:28 – Thomas confessed Him to be Lord and God. Jesus was God in the flesh, the only-begotten Son having all characteristics of Deity, unique in His relation to God. (John 1:1-3,14)

So, when people confess Jesus today, they should mean that He is the Son of God, who partakes of the nature of Deity.

(Compare 1 John 4:2,5; John 11:27; 1:34; Matthew 3:17; 17:5; 14:33; 26:63,64; Acts 8:37; 2 John 7.)

Confess Jesus as Savior

John 4:42 – After the Samaritans met Jesus, they said they believed that Jesus was indeed the Christ, the **Savior** of the world.

Jesus is the One who died on the cross as the sacrifice for our sins. As a result, all men can have hope of salvation from sin. Without Him, there would be no hope.

(Acts 4:12; Romans 10:9; Philippians 2:11)

Confess Jesus as Lord

Romans 10:9,10 – To be saved we must confess the **Lord** Jesus ("Jesus as Lord" – ASV). "Lord" means master or ruler – one whom everyone ought to obey. Faith is a conviction in the heart, but confession is here listed separately from faith. This confession should be made with the **mouth.** Every Bible example of confession involves something a person **says.** (Compare Philippians 2:11.)

Luke 6:46 – Why **call** (confess) Jesus "Lord" if you don't **do** what He says? It does no good to call Jesus "Lord" and not obey. Nor is it enough to change our way of living while refusing to confess Him. Both are required.

To confess Jesus as Lord is to make a pledge of allegiance to His authority. You are calling upon Jesus as **your** Lord – the one **you** must obey. A person cannot make a Scriptural confession if he does not believe in Jesus or if he has not truly repented and determined to **obey** Jesus.

(Hebrews 4:14; 10:23; Matthew 7:21; John 20:28)

Conclusions about what it means to confess Christ:

Confession of Christ is a statement made with the **mouth** about **Jesus.**

Since there is some variation in the way confession is worded, we conclude the Scripture does not bind one set formula of words. Scriptural confession does not consist of reciting a word-for-word quotation. It requires understanding concepts about who Jesus is and then conveying by mouth that we accept those concepts as true.

Essentially, one confesses Jesus to be all that the Bible claims Him to be. He professes that He believes Jesus to be God's Divine Son, the anointed ruler of God's people, the Savior of the world, and the Master whom we all must obey. In saying this, one admits that he must live his life in total obedience to Jesus' will. This is what we must understand and intend to convey to others by our confession.

Have you confessed Jesus to be what the Bible teaches that He is?

(Note that confession can be done in answer to questions – Matthew 27:11; John 9:35-38.)

When Should One Confess Christ?

In a sense, we should confess Christ repeatedly throughout our lives as Christians. But we are discussing the confession required as part of conversion, becoming a Christian. Surely this confession must come **after one believes and repents**, for otherwise it would not be a true confession.

But must one confess Christ as a necessary step in order to be forgiven of sins and become Jesus' disciple? Does one confess that God **has** forgiven his sins, or must one confess **before** his sins are forgiven? Consider the following evidence:

Examples During Jesus' Life

During Jesus' lifetime a pattern was established that a person must confess Him in order to be His disciple. Since this occurred before Jesus' death, the terms of the New Testament were not yet in effect, nor did people enter Jesus' church at that time. Nevertheless, **confession was a test of who was or was not a disciple**.

Matthew 3:16,17; 17:5 – The heavenly Father Himself set the pattern by confessing Jesus to be His Son both at Jesus' baptism and at the Transfiguration.

John 1:49 – Nathanael, when he first believed, confessed Jesus to be the Son of God, King of Israel.

John 4:42 – The Samaritans, when they first believed, confessed Jesus to be the Savior of the world.

John 9:35-38 – Jesus healed a blind man. Later, when Jesus affirmed that He was the Son of God, the blind man confessed, "I believe." (Note that confession occurred in response to Jesus' prompting.)

Matthew 10:32,33 – Whoever confesses Jesus before men, Jesus will confess him before the Father. Confession of Jesus is a condition of fellowship. Confession must continue after one is a disciple, but fellowship cannot **begin** for those who will not confess.

John 12:42,43 – An example of **non-confession.** Certain Jews believed in Jesus but would not confess Him. Surely no one would affirm that they were disciples. So, **confession was a test of discipleship** during Jesus' lifetime. It stood between discipleship and non-discipleship. The Jews recognized this, for they cast out of the synagogue those who confessed (compare 9:22).

So, people confessed Christ when they wanted to become disciples. And if people would **not** confess, they were **not** disciples even though they believed. So, confession was a condition to discipleship.

Salvation through Jesus Christ

Disciples were later called "Christians" (Acts 11:26). So, we would expect the pattern to continue: in order to become a Christian, one first had to confess Christ.

Romans 10:9,10

With the mouth confession is "unto salvation" ("to salvation" – NKJV). So, confession is a necessary condition to salvation from sin. Confession comes first, then comes salvation.

But sins are actually forgiven when people are baptized, not before (Acts 2:38; 22:16; Mark 16:16; Romans 6:3,4; Galatians 3:27). Since confession must come before salvation, and since people are forgiven at the point of baptism, it follows that confession must come before baptism. *

1 Timothy 6:12,13

Note some translations of these verses:

NKJV – "...lay hold on eternal life, to which you were also called and have confessed the good confession in the presence of many witnesses."

NASB – "...take hold of the eternal life to which you were called, and you made the good confession..."

NIV – "Take hold of the eternal life to which you were called when you made your good confession..."

Timothy made the "good confession" when he was **called** to eternal life. Paul is writing to Timothy to urge him to **continue** fighting the good fight, so he will eventually receive that eternal life.

What is the "good confession"?

Verse 13 says this was the same confession Jesus made before Pilate. As already mentioned, before Pilate Jesus acknowledged He was King, anointed Ruler of God's people: the Christ. So, when Timothy was called to eternal life, he confessed like Jesus confessed Himself before Pilate.

2 Thessalonians 2:14 – We are called for salvation by the gospel. Timothy was called by the gospel so he could have the hope of eternal life. When Timothy received that call, he responded by **confessing the good confession.** The time to confess, then, is when we are called by the gospel to eternal life and accept it to be true.

Just as confession was a test of discipleship while Jesus lived on earth, so confession was a requirement to salvation after Jesus' death. (Compare Hebrews 10:22,23.)

Acts 8:36-38

The treasurer confessed Jesus before he was baptized.

When Philip taught the treasurer about Jesus, he wanted to be baptized. But Philip said he first had to believe. So Philip would know the treasurer believed, the treasurer confessed that he believed in Jesus.

We have studied many passages showing that confession is essential in order for one to be forgiven of sins. This means that confession must come after belief and repentance but before baptism. This example shows that these conclusions are correct, for this is exactly what happened in this case.

What about the fact that verse 37 is not found in some ancient manuscripts so is not in some modern translations?

* Almost without exception, translations include verse 37 either in the text or in the footnotes.

* All reliable textual critics agree that the **doctrine** of Scripture is not changed by questions about what belongs in the text. It follows that, whether or not one thinks verse 37 belongs in the text, he must acknowledge that **what the verse teaches is true**.

* God has promised to preserve His truth in the Scriptures for all ages (Psalm 119:152,160; Isaiah 40:8; 30:8; John 12:48; 2 John 2; 1 Peter 1:23-25; 2 Peter 1:12-15; 2 Timothy 3:16,17). Until the late 1800s all English Bibles included Acts 8:37. Would God have fulfilled His promise to preserve the truth if He allowed a verse to be included that taught error for all these years? Again, whether or not we agree that the verse is authentic, we must all admit that what it teaches is true.

For further discussion of the preservation of Scripture, see our article on that subject on our Bible Instruction web site at www.gospelway.com/instruct/.

1 John 4:15

Whoever confesses Jesus is the Son of God, **God dwells in him** and he in God. As we have repeatedly seen, confession of Jesus is a condition of fellowship with God. Some such verses teach that we must continue to confess Jesus after conversion. But since confession is essential to fellowship, it necessarily follows that fellowship cannot **begin** until we have confessed. (Hebrews 10:22,23)

Like Bible study, faith, and repentance, confession is a requirement that must continue after we are converted. But since all of them are essential to salvation, it follows that all must **begin** before baptism.

What about you? Have you confessed Christ as a condition of your salvation?

Why Should One Confess Christ?

Let us summarize the evidence that confession is a condition essential to receive salvation and become a child of God.

Matthew 10:32,33 – Jesus will confess before the Father those who confess Him before men. It follows that those who want to be confessed before the Father must confess Jesus, and those have not confessed Jesus have not been confessed before the Father.

Romans 10:9,10 – In order to be saved, we must believe and confess. Just as Mark 16:16 teaches that belief and baptism are essential to salvation, and Acts 2:38 teaches that repentance and baptism are for (unto) remission of sins, so Romans 10:9,10 teaches that faith and confession are necessary to salvation.

1 Timothy 6:12,13 – Like Timothy, people who want eternal life must confess Christ when they are called by the gospel.

Acts 8:37 – Before one can be **baptized** he must confess Jesus. But remember that baptism is necessary to salvation. So one must confess before he can be baptized for remission of sins.

John 12:42 – People who do not confess are not disciples, therefore confession is essential in order for one to **become a disciple**. (Compare John 9:35-38.)

1 John 4:15 – Whoever confesses Jesus is the Son of God, **God dwells in him** and he in God. It follows that God does not begin to dwell in a sinner until he has confessed Christ.

Conclusion

Have you properly and scripturally confessed Christ?

Confession must be based on a **proper understanding and belief** about Jesus. Do you believe Jesus is all that the gospel claims Him to be?

Confession must be based on **repentance and commitment to obey Jesus** as the absolute Lord and Master of your life.

After you confess Christ, you should be **baptized** so your sins can be forgiven. Then you must follow through on the commitment you have confessed and live a life of faithful service, continuing to confess Christ throughout your life.

Have you confessed Christ and received salvation by His blood? Are you continuing to live faithfully confessing Christ to others as you have opportunity?

* The context of Romans 10 refers to unbelievers who need to be saved (9:30-33; 10:1,4,6,8,11,14,16,17). Specifically, verses 13,14 describe people who have **not heard or believed**, but then they hear, believe, call on the Lord, and are **saved**. Verses 9,10 show that confession, like faith, is essential to receive salvation. (Also, compare verse 13 to Acts 2:21,36-38, where the context teaches unbelieving Jews how to be saved.)

Why does Paul say "you" in Romans 10:9,10 when addressing saved Romans? He is continuing a line of thought from the preceding verses that quote Old Testament verses that refer to "you." Paul speaks *to* saved people but discusses passages that speak *about* unsaved people who need to receive salvation.

The Action of Baptism

Introduction:

The purpose of this study is to consider the action involved in baptism. Physically, what should be done when one is baptized?

Let us start by considering some quotations about the subject. Please consider carefully what people of different religious groups say:

Different Views about the Issue

Some Denominations View This as a Matter of Choice.

"Baptism may be administered by sprinkling, pouring, or immersion, according to the choice of the applicant." – *Church of the Nazarene Manual,* 1972 ed., page 33

"What is the meaning of the word 'baptize'? 'Baptize' means to apply water by washing, pouring, sprinkling, or immersing." – *Luther's Small Catechism,* par. 244, page 170

"Dipping of the person into the water is not necessary; the Baptism is rightly administered by pouring or sprinkling water upon the person" – "Westminster Confession of Faith," par. 6.141, *Presbyterian Book of Confessions,* 1967 ed.

"How is baptism given? It is given by pouring water over the forehead of the person to be baptized ..." – A Catechism for Adults (Catholic), 1975 ed., page 63

So some churches sprinkle or pour water on the person's head. Most churches say there are several acceptable choices regarding the action involved in baptism. Others say only immersion is acceptable.

Some Leaders of the Above Denominations Admit Immersion Is the Biblical Teaching.

"Luther urged, in opposition to the standard practice of pouring, that baptism should be by immersion. He pointed out that the word in the Greek language means 'To plunge something entirely into the water, so that the water closes over it,' and urged that immersion should be the mode of baptism. Today, however, the general practice of the Lutheran Church is to administer baptism by pouring, although immersion is also permitted" – *A Compend of Luther's Theology*, p. 167, via *Handbook of Religious Quotations*, p. 11.

Luther is also quoted as saying:

"The term baptism is a Greek word; it may be rendered into Latin by MERSIO – when we immerse anything in water, that it may be entirely covered with water. And though this custom be quite abolished among the generality (for neither do they entirely dip children, but only sprinkle them with a little water), nevertheless they ought to be wholly immersed, and immediately drawn out again, for the etymology of the word seems to require it." – quoted by Brents in *Gospel Plan of Salvation*, page 280.

John Calvin stated: "The word baptize signifies to immerse, and the rite of immersion was practiced by the ancient church." – quoted by Brents, pages 230, 231

"In Apostolic times the body of the baptized person was immersed, for St. Paul looks on this immersion as typifying burial with Christ, and speaks of baptism as a bath ... [But the belief] that baptism can be validly given by immersion, infusion, or aspersion, is fully justified by tradition ... Anciently ... baptism was constantly given to adults and the rite of immersion prevailed ..." – *The Catholic Dictionary* on "baptism" and "baptistery," pages 60-64

These quotations do not constitute conclusive evidence of the action of baptism, but should give people who practice sprinkling or pouring cause to consider the question we are studying. These prominent leaders in their churches all agree that immersion is the action of baptism taught in the Bible and practiced by the apostles, so those who practice sprinkling or pouring are following tradition or some authority other than the Bible.

Definitions of the Word "Baptize"

Some modern dictionaries claim baptism can mean sprinkling, pouring, or immersion.

But modern dictionaries just define how the word is used today. This does not prove what the word meant in the language of the Bible. Even our English words change meaning over time (consider how the word "gay" has changed in recent years). So what does "baptism" mean in the **Bible**?

Most modern dictionaries also explain the **origin** of words. They show that "baptize" comes from a **Greek** word meaning "to immerse" (*Random House College Dictionary*). This is the meaning used in the New Testament, which was written in Greek. By looking in your English dictionary for the **original** meaning of the word, you can confirm for yourself that "baptize," in the language in which the Bible was written, originally meant to immerse or dip or plunge.

Dictionaries of Bible words show "baptize" means to immerse.

Thayer's lexicon on βαπτιζω says: "to dip, immerge, submerge." Many other dictionaries show the basic, root meaning of the Bible word is to immerse. (See Vine, Arndt and Gingrich, etc.)

(Remember, these dictionaries were often written by members of churches that practice sprinkling and pouring. We would expect them to define the words in a way that defended their church practice, if they could have done so.)

The Modern Literal Version consistently translates the original Greek word as "immerse" or "immersion" in Acts 2:38; 22:16; Mark 16:16; 1 Peter 3:21; etc.

The Greek language, in which the Bible was written, had other words for "sprinkle" or "pour":

Sprinkle (ραντιζω) – Animal blood and water was "sprinkled" in Old Testament purification rites (Hebrews 9:13).

Pour (χεω and variant forms) – Jesus "poured" out the changers' money (John 2:15).

Had God wanted to authorize sprinkling and pouring for baptism, these words were available; but instead He repeatedly and consistently chose a word that never means sprinkle or pour.

The Bible word for "baptism" means immersion, not sprinkling or pouring. But most people cannot study Greek to prove this. And dictionaries are written by fallible men. So we still need to search further. But surely we have reason to suspect modern sprinkling and pouring may not be correct.

Only the Bible Can Give a Conclusive Answer to This Question.

Matthew 28:18-20 – Jesus' command to be baptized is based on His authority over heaven and earth.

2 Timothy 3:16,17 – The Scriptures instruct us in righteousness and provide us to all good works. (James 1:25; 2 Peter 1:3; Ephesians 3:3-5)

Matthew 15:9 – Following the doctrines of men in such matters makes our worship vain.

Galatians 1:8,9 – Anyone who preaches differently from the gospel is accursed.

This issue must be settled on the basis of Bible teaching, not on human creeds or church traditions.

Note that we do not need a verse that expressly says, "Do not sprinkle or pour." If the Bible teaches us to immerse and never authorizes sprinkling or pouring, then the latter should be rejected as being human in origin and different from the gospel.

(See also 2 John 9-11; Colossians 3:17; Jeremiah 10:23; Proverbs 14:12; 3:5,6; Revelation 22:18,19; 1 Timothy 1:3; 2 Timothy 1:13.)

The Bible Evidence

The best way to understand a Bible command is to study the passages that refer to it in context, comparing them to other passages on the subject. This is especially how we learn the meaning of words.

Notice what baptism requires in the Bible and consider what action fits what the Bible says.

Water

The element or substance used is not inherent in the word "baptize." But the element used in the baptism of the Great Commission – the baptism Jesus commanded everyone to receive – is water.

Acts 10:47,48 – "Can anyone forbid **water**, that these should not be baptized…" The command to be baptized refers to baptism in water.

Suppose someone wanted to baptize people in rose petals. Would that be obeying the command, or would that be changing it and following human doctrine? Note that no passage expressly says not to use rose petals, yet that would violate Scripture because it differs from what the gospel teaches.

Other verses listed below also show the element in baptism should be water.

Much Water

John 3:23 – John baptized near Salim because there was **much water** there. So baptism involves the use of "much water."

Do sprinkling or pouring require much water? No! Baptism according to the Bible requires "much water," but sprinkling and pouring do not require much water.

Does immersion require much water? Yes, it requires enough to immerse someone in.

So Bible baptism requires "much water." Immersion fits, because it requires much water. Sprinkling and pouring do not fit, because they do not require much water. This helps us understand the meaning of "baptism" in the New Testament.

Coming to the Water

Acts 8:36-39 – Philip and the eunuch **came to** water (verse 36), then the eunuch was baptized.

Some folks think the eunuch pulled out a bottle of water and Philip used some of it to baptize him. Not so! The eunuch was baptized in a body of water they came to as they traveled. Other Bible examples also confirm that people who were baptized went to the water. (See John 3:23; Mark 1:9; etc.)

When people receive sprinkling or pouring, do they need to go to the water? No, the water can be brought to them, because not much is required.

When people are immersed, do they need to go to the water? Yes.

Again, immersion fits the Bible description of baptism. Sprinkling and pouring do not fit.

Going Down into the Water

Bible baptism involves going down into the water.

Acts 8:38 – Philip and the eunuch **went down into** the water and he baptized him. This shows why baptism involves "much water" – it must be enough for people to go down into!

When denominations practice sprinkling or pouring, does the person go down into the water? No. But Bible baptism requires going down into the water.

When a person is immersed, must the person go down into the water? Yes, so immersion fits the Bible description of baptism, but sprinkling and pouring do not fit.

But some folks claim you can "go down into the water" and then sprinkle or pour water on the person.

This is how artist's conceptions sometimes picture Jesus' baptism.

But is this the way denominations baptize people? Does the person go down into the water, then water is sprinkled on him? No! I am always amazed when people argue that some practice **could** be done, when they are not doing it! This "argument" does not defend what denominations practice, so why use it?

Why don't denominational preachers take the candidate down into the water to sprinkle or pour? Because it does not make sense to go to all the trouble. And it would not have made sense in Bible times either. If Bible baptism was sprinkling or pouring, preachers would have done what preachers do today when they sprinkle or pour.

Bible examples help us see what "baptism" means. The fact is that, when denominations sprinkle or pour, they do not do what the Bible says baptism involves. Only immersion fits the description.

Coming Up Out of the Water

Acts 8:39 – After the eunuch had been baptized, he **came up out** of the water. In order to come up out of the water, he first had to be down in the water.

Mark 1:9,10 – Jesus was baptized "in" the Jordan River, then **came up from** ("out of" – footnote) the water.

When denominations sprinkle or pour, does the person then come up out of (or from) the water? No, because they never went down into it!

When people are immersed, do they come up out of the water? Yes!

Bible baptism requires coming to the water, going down into it, and coming up out of it. None of these are required by sprinkling or pouring, but immersion requires all of them. Immersion fits the pattern of Bible baptism, but sprinkling and pouring do not.

A Burial

Colossians 2:12 – Buried with Him in baptism in which you also were raised with Him.

In baptism we are **buried** with Jesus and raised with Him. As He was buried in the earth, so we are buried in baptism.

Are people buried and raised in sprinkling or pouring? When Jesus was buried, did they sprinkle a little dirt on Him, like folks do in sprinkling or pouring?

Matthew 12:40 – He was buried in the heart of the earth.

Matthew 27:60,66 – He was laid in a tomb hewn out of rock and a great stone covered the opening. He was completely enclosed in the element.

In baptism we are buried (completely enclosed and surrounded) in water, as Jesus was buried in the earth.

Romans 6:4 – We are buried with Him by baptism.

Some say baptism is "just a symbol" of Jesus' burial, so it does not matter how it is done. There is a symbolic element in baptism, but how does that prove that the action does not matter?

Do the passages say Jesus was buried, but we don't need to be buried?

It says **we** are **buried** and **we** are **raised** in baptism. The one to be baptized must be buried and raised. When denominations sprinkle or pour, is the person himself buried and raised? No. In immersion is the person buried and raised? Yes!

We have no right to change the symbols that God commands us to use.

In the Lord's Supper, Jesus authorized bread and fruit of the vine as symbols of Jesus' flesh and blood. This involves symbolism, but may we say the symbols do not matter so we may use hamburger and Coke?

Also, in baptism we are buried in water. If symbols don't matter, may we use milk or rose petals?

When God commands actions, even if they involve symbolism, we must respect the act as God commanded it instead of changing it. Baptism involves a burial and a resurrection like Jesus' burial and resurrection. Immersion fits the command as God ordained it. How can sprinkling or pouring symbolize a burial and a resurrection?

If we change God's command and sprinkle or pour water on people instead of burying them in baptism, then we may as well use hamburger and Coke in communion and baptize people in rose petals. But if we do, we violate Matthew 15:9, Galatians 1:8,9, and all the passages we have cited that show we must do what the Lord says instead of following human changes.

The fact remains that immersion fits the Bible description of baptism. Sprinkling and pouring do not fit.

A Resurrection

The same passages that say we are buried in baptism also say we are raised in baptism.

Colossians 2:12 – Buried with Him in baptism in which you also were **raised** with Him.

Romans 6:4 – Just as Christ was **raised** from the dead by the glory of the Father, even so we also should walk in newness of life.

Sprinkling and pouring are not Scriptural baptism, because they involve neither a burial nor a resurrection. Only immersion fits.

A Washing of the Body

Hebrews 10:22 – We have our hearts sprinkled from an evil conscience and our **bodies washed** with pure water. Note the contrast between the sprinkling of the heart and the washing of the body.

The blood of Jesus is sprinkled on our heart to cleanse us from sin. This must be spiritual, since it cannot be physical. (Hebrews 9:14)

But what is washed with water? The **body**! Clearly, this refers to baptism. Just as with the Lord's Supper, baptism involves both an inner meaning and an outer action. In baptism the heart is cleansed of sin when the body is washed in baptism.

2 Kings 5:10-14 – Elisha told Naaman to wash seven times in the Jordan river to be cleansed of his leprosy. The passage says that Naaman "dipped" in the river and was cleansed. The word for "dipped" in the Septuagint Greek translation is the same Greek word used in the New Testament for baptism.

This shows that, properly translated, the Greek word for baptism means to dip. Furthermore, the example of Naaman shows that, when God commands a person to wash his body in water to be cleansed, the command is obeyed by dipping in the water. So, when Hebrews 10:22 instructs us to wash our bodies, this is done by dipping in water – that is by baptism, a complete immersion.

Denominations sprinkle or pour water on the head. But Bible baptism involves washing the body. In immersion, the body is washed. Immersion fits the Bible descriptions of baptism. Sprinkling and pouring do not fit.

Conclusion

Scriptural baptism requires all the following:

* Water
* Much water
* Coming to the water
* Going down into the water
* Coming up out of the water
* Burial
* Resurrection
* Washing the body

Sprinkling and pouring fit only the first point (water); they do not fit any of the other points. Only immersion fits the Bible description of baptism.

No other form or action is acceptable.

Sprinkling and pouring are human in origin. They are changes from God's plan. Only complete immersion can be practiced according to Jesus' authority.

Gospel baptism is immersion, not sprinkling or pouring. If you have not been immersed in baptism, then you have not obeyed Jesus' command! You have followed only the doctrine of men.

If you now wish to obey Jesus, you must do what He said to do: be baptized (immersed) as described in the passages studied above.

He who believes and is baptized will be saved – Mark 16:16.

Should Babies Be Baptized?

Introduction:

Jesus clearly commanded people to be baptized (Matthew 28:18-20), yet there is much disagreement about *who* should be baptized.

Some religious groups baptize babies. But others say that, before one is baptized, a person should be old enough to accept the responsibility to make his own decision whether or not to be baptized and to live the Christian life. The purpose of this study is to learn what the Bible says about this subject.

We begin with an important basic principle:

God approves of religious practices only if He has authorized them in the New Testament.

The Scriptures provide us to all good works (2 Timothy 3:16,17). So, if a practice is not included in God's word, it must not be a good work. If a practice is not authorized in the New Testament, then it must be human in origin; God says He will not accept it (2 John 9; Galatians 1:6-9; Matthew 15:9; Proverbs 14:12; etc.). So, everything we do in religion must be done by Jesus' authority (Colossians 3:17).

According to these Scriptures we should practice infant baptism only if we can find statements in the New Testament that show that God wants us to practice it. To know that infant baptism is unacceptable, we do not need to find a passage that expressly forbids the practice. Rather, if the Bible tells us specifically who to baptize, and if infants are not included in those instructions, then we should abandon the practice of baptizing babies.

Please consider the following Bible teaching:

Can Babies Meet the Conditions that Must Precede Baptism?

The Bible reveals that a person must do certain things before he can be baptized. If these things are not done, then the baptism would not be acceptable to God. So we ask whether or not a baby can fulfill the Scriptural prerequisites of baptism.

Note that God is no respecter of persons (Acts 10:34,35; Romans 2:11). He did not give two sets of prerequisites for baptism: one for babies and one for adults. Whatever the Bible requires of some people to be baptized, it requires the same of all people.

Before Baptism One Must Hear and Understand the Gospel.

Mark 16:15,16 – Before anyone can be baptized, the gospel must first be preached to him. But what good would it do to preach to a baby?

John 6:44,45 – No one can come to Jesus until he has been taught from the Father. He must "learn" and understand the meaning of what is being taught. Can babies do this? (Compare 1 Corinthians 14:20.)

Acts 2:36,41 – The first gospel sermon demonstrates what it means for people to learn the gospel. Peter taught the people evidence that Jesus is God's Son so they would "know assuredly" that Jesus is Lord and Christ (verses 14-36). Those who gladly received this message were then baptized (verse 41). Can babies hear, learn, and gladly receive the gospel message?

Before Baptism One Must Believe the Gospel.

Mark 16:15,16 – Every creature who is baptized must first believe the gospel. The command to be baptized applies only to those who hear, understand, and believe the gospel. Can a baby do these things?

Galatians 3:26,27 – All people, who are baptized, must do so by faith. Before anyone is baptized, he must first understand the gospel well enough to believe it.

Acts 8:12 – The men and women of Samaria gave heed to the gospel that was preached (verses 5,6) and were then baptized. When were they baptized? When they believed, not before. Can babies believe? If not, they should not be baptized until they do believe.

In all Bible examples, people were baptized only when they personally possessed faith based on their own understanding of the gospel. Never were people baptized on the basis of someone else's faith,

Salvation through Jesus Christ

such as their parents' faith. No one else can believe for us, just like no one else can be baptized for us.
(See also Acts 8:36-39; 18:8; Romans 1:16; 10:13-17.)

Before Baptism One Must Repent of Sins.

Acts 2:38 – Before being baptized, every person ("every one of you") must first repent. Repentance is a change of mind: a decision to turn from sin and begin to live for God (compare Matthew 21:28,29). This decision involves a commitment to put God first and to live all our lives faithfully serving Him.

Note that the person who is baptized must himself first repent. This requires a personal choice. No one else can make this decision for us. Can a baby make this choice?

Some people claim that "children" in verse 39 means babies are included among those to whom this "promise" was made. But "children" simply means offspring, regardless of age (note Matthew 3:9; 10:21; 21:28; John 8:39). I have three children, all of whom are grown and have children of their own; but they are still my "children."

The "promise" here is for those who repent and are baptized (verse 38). But babies cannot repent, nor can they do other things required in the context (verses 36,40,41,42). So, the "promise" to the "children" was fulfilled when they were old enough to do what God requires, not while they were babies.
(See also 2 Corinthians 7:10; Mark 1:4,5.)

Before Baptism One Must Confess Christ.

Romans 10:9,10 – To be saved, one must believe in his heart and confess Christ with his mouth. How can a baby confess Christ with its mouth when it cannot even speak?

Acts 8:35-39 – Here is an example of confession before baptism. The candidate for baptism must state that he believes so that the one who baptizes him/her understands that he is baptizing someone who does have faith. Babies cannot communicate regarding their faith in any understandable way, therefore it is not Scriptural to baptize them.

Churches that practice infant baptism also commonly practice "confirmation." The purpose of confirmation is so that people, who were baptized as babies, can publicly "confirm" their faith when they are old enough to understand and make their own choice about serving God. The very existence of such a practice is an admission that the child did **not** understand, believe, and repent before he was baptized. But people who do not meet these prerequisites should not even be baptized!

We have now learned four things that the Bible requires every person to personally do before he can be baptized. Before anyone can be baptized, he must hear and understand the gospel, believe it, repent of sins, and confess Christ. God is no respecter of persons, so the plan is the same for everyone. But little babies cannot do any of these things. Therefore, the command to be baptized is not addressed to them. To baptize them anyway would be acting without God's authority. It would be doing something different from what God says must be done.

Can Babies Be Baptized for the Right Reason?

Each Individual Must Obey God from Proper Motives.

Romans 6:17,18 – To be freed from sin, one must obey from the **heart** the teaching delivered. This obedience includes baptism (verses 3,4). God is pleased only when we serve Him from the willing choice of our own hearts. Our acts of service are valueless if others force them upon us against our will or without our consent.

Acts 2:40,41 – Those who **gladly received** the message were baptized. Each individual personally made his own decision to be baptized. No one else can be baptized for us, and no one else can make that choice for us. A person who has not gladly received the message in his own heart should not be baptized.

Other people may teach and encourage us to obey God, but they cannot decide for us whether or not we will be baptized. Since a baby cannot possibly make this decision and cannot communicate any such decision to others, to baptize it anyway would violate God's law of personal responsibility.

(See also the notes below on Ezekiel 18:20 and 2 Corinthians 5:10. Compare Romans 2:28,29; 1 Peter 1:22; 3:21; 2 Corinthians 8:5; Revelation 22:17; Philippians 2:12; 1 Corinthians 13:1-3.)

Each Person Should Be Baptized for the Purpose of Receiving Forgiveness.

Again, since God is no respecter of persons, the purpose of baptism must be the same for all who are baptized. He did not give two different purposes, one for adults and another for babies. What are the proper purposes for which all must be baptized?

Mark 16:16 – He who believes and is baptized will be saved.

Acts 2:38 – Repent and be baptized for the remission of sins.

Acts 22:16 – Be baptized and wash away your sins.

1 Peter 3:21 – Baptism also now saves us.

So the person who is baptized must do it for the purpose of being forgiven or saved from his sins. And we have already learned that baptism pleases God only if it is offered from the right motive and purpose.

In the Lord's Supper, as an illustration, a person displeases God even if he does the right actions, but his reasons are wrong (1 Corinthians 11:23-29). Likewise, if a person is baptized but does not do it to receive forgiveness of sins, then the baptism is not proper. But a baby cannot understand the meaning of baptism, so how can he be baptized from a proper motive?

A Baby Cannot Be Baptized to Receive Forgiveness, Because It Has No Sins.

Since baptism must be done for the purpose of receiving forgiveness of sins, a baby could Scripturally be baptized only if it was guilty of sins. But is a baby guilty of sin?

How could a baby become guilty of sin?

We become sinners when we transgress God's law (1 John 3:4; James 1:13-15; Isaiah 59:1,2). But a baby cannot understand God's law, so how could it be held accountable for violating it?

Some people say that babies need baptism because they have inherited guilt from Adam. However:

Ezekiel 18:20 – The child does not bear the iniquity of the father; the wickedness of the wicked is upon himself and the righteousness of the righteous is upon himself. The only person held accountable for Adam's sin is Adam, not his descendants.

2 Corinthians 5:10 – Each one will be judged according to what **he** has done in the body, good or bad. So, no one will be condemned for Adam's sin, except Adam!

This also confirms that no one will be justified because someone else decided to do good: the righteousness of the righteous is upon himself. So, a child is not a sinner because his ancestors sinned, nor is he made righteous because his parents decide to have him baptized. Each person will be judged for what he chooses to do, not for what others choose to do.

Further, the Bible says that Jesus was without sin (Hebrews 2:14,17; 2 Corinthians 5:21; 1 John 3:5). Since He was born a descendant of Adam, how could He have been without sin if babies inherit the guilt of Adam's sin? And if He did not inherit guilt from Adam, why would we?

If a baby is guilty of sin, what happens if it dies without being baptized?

Since baptism is necessary to forgiveness of sins, if a baby dies without baptism, wouldn't it follow that the baby is eternally lost? Almost no one will accept this conclusion, yet to deny the conclusion is to admit that babies are not really guilty of sin.

Further, if a baby must be baptized to be saved, then it must rely entirely on its parents to choose to baptize it. It has no choice in determining its own eternal destiny. This contradicts all the scriptures we have quoted showing that salvation is a matter of individual choice (2 Corinthians 5:10; etc.).

Since salvation is a matter of individual choice, and since a baby cannot choose or express a choice to be baptized, we conclude that the baby is not lost to begin with. So, it does not need baptism.

What is the spiritual condition of a baby?

Since babies have committed no sin and have inherited no sin, it follows that they must be innocent. Notice other Scriptures that confirm this conclusion:

Psalms 106:37,38; Jeremiah 19:4,5 – Babies sacrificed to idols were "innocent."

Hebrews 12:9 – Earthly fathers are fathers of our *flesh*, but God is the Father of our *spirits*. Adam was a father of our flesh, not of our spirit, so Adam cannot give us a defiled spirit. Since God is the Father of our spirits, would the sinless, righteous God give us sinful spirits? (Zechariah 12:1; Ecclesiastes 12:7)

Matthew 19:14; 18:3 – To enter the kingdom, we must be converted and become like little children. If children are sinners, would this not mean that we must be converted and become like little sinners? Other passages show that we must become innocent or cleansed of sin to enter the kingdom (Colossians 1:13,14). So, becoming like little children must mean, among other things, that children are innocent; we become like them by being forgiven of sin so we can enter the kingdom.

Some people say these verses mean we should baptize babies so they can come to Jesus. But Jesus did not **baptize** the babies who came to Him. They came so He could touch them and pray for them (Matthew 19:13; Mark 10:13-16), not so He could baptize them. They were acceptable to Jesus just as they were, without baptism.

A baby does not need forgiveness for the simple reason that he is not guilty. He is in a safe condition, not accountable for sin until he is old enough to be able to understand and accept the responsibility to obey God. Since baptism is for the remission of sins, and since a baby has no sins, it follows that babies do not need baptism.

Some people admit that babies have no sin, but they baptize them, not for forgiveness, but just as a "dedication." But remember that the gospel says the purpose of baptism is to receive remission of sins, and it must be done for that purpose. Baptism of babies as a "dedication," not for forgiveness, constitutes a human invention that perverts the Scriptural purpose of baptism.

So, no matter how you look at it, infant baptism perverts the purpose of baptism.

Can Babies Fulfill the Requirements that Follow Baptism?

When a person is baptized, he makes a commitment to live the rest of his life according to the Bible. He must then accept certain responsibilities that the gospel requires of all baptized people. Some young people wonder whether or not they are ready to be baptized. No one is ready to be baptized until he or she is able and willing to accept these responsibilities.

Here are a few of the responsibilities that God requires of all baptized people. Can babies do these?

All Baptized People Should Accept the Responsibilities of Church Membership.

1 Corinthians 12:13,25,26 – Baptism makes people members of Jesus' body, which is the church (Ephesians 1:22,23; 5:23). Churches that baptize babies often do not consider them to be church members. But God's word says that, when one has been baptized, he is automatically in the church.

All members of the church should then care for, suffer with, and rejoice with other members. Can a baby do this? (Compare Hebrews 10:22-25.)

All Baptized People Should Exhort and Encourage Other Christians.

Ephesians 4:16 – In the body (the church) every joint and each part should work to edify and build up the body. What work can babies do? None. Therefore, they should not be baptized into the body.

All Baptized People Should Worship God.

Acts 2:38-42,47 – Again, the Lord adds all baptized people to His church (verses 41,47). To baptize people, without viewing them as fully members of the church, would be unscriptural. These baptized people then continued in the acts of worship: breaking bread, prayer, the apostles' doctrine, etc. Can babies do this?

1 Corinthians 14:15-20 – Members of the church (which includes all baptized people – 12:13) should assemble with other Christians to sing, pray, and teach. All this should be done with understanding. But verse 20 expressly says that babies cannot do these things with the understanding that God requires.

1 Corinthians 10:16,17; 11:23-29 – All members of the body should eat and drink the Lord's Supper remembering and discerning the meaning of Jesus' death. If they eat without understanding, they eat and drink damnation to themselves (11:23-29). Can babies eat, drink,

remember, and discern the Lord's death? If not, they should not be baptized into the body!

Notice carefully: God requires all church members to worship Him with understanding. Babies cannot understand. So, babies should not be baptized into the church! The command to be baptized is not addressed to babies and does not include them.

Baptized People Should Put God First in Their Lives.

Romans 6:3,4,11-18 – When people are baptized, they should walk in newness of life. They must not let sin reign in their bodies, but must use their members as instruments of righteousness. No one should be baptized until they are able and ready to accept this responsibility from their own hearts.

Romans 12:1,2 – Those who are "brethren" (people who entered God's family at the point of baptism) should present their bodies as living sacrifices to God, not being conformed to the world. Everyone who is baptized must accept this commitment. Can babies make such a commitment?

1 Corinthians 15:58 – Brethren (i.e., children of God) should be steadfast, immovable, always abounding in the Lord's work. No one should be baptized till he chooses for himself to work for the Lord.

Matthew 28:19,20 – Baptized people should be taught to obey **all** Jesus' commands. This shows that people need not know all God's commands at the time they are baptized. But they must be **capable** of learning and applying those commands. And they must have a heart willing to accept and obey everything Jesus says to do.

Every person must make these commitments at baptism. A baby cannot do this, so he should not be baptized until he is old enough to choose for himself to do so. Furthermore, these are the responsibilities young people should understand and be willing to accept before they are ready to be baptized.

Note carefully that we have learned what God says people must do **before** they can be baptized, **during** baptism (the proper purpose), and **after** baptism. Babies do not qualify in any of these areas. To baptize babies, then, would be to act by human authority without God's authority, thereby violating the will of God.

What Evidence Is Offered to Defend Infant Baptism?

Remember that practices displease God unless they are authorized in His word. We have given evidence that shows babies cannot meet necessary conditions to be baptized. Yet some folks attempt to offer

Bible proof for infant baptism. We have answered several such efforts already. Let us notice others.

Babies with Faith

Some say babies should be baptized because they can believe. But remember that denominations typically baptize babies as young as a few days or a few weeks old. Can anyone seriously believe that babies that young can have the kind of faith the Bible requires before baptism?

Romans 10:13-17 – Faith comes by hearing God's word.

The only way anyone can have faith is by being taught God's word. Do churches teach little babies the gospel before baptizing them? If not, then they are baptizing people who have no faith.

Instead, denominations try to instill faith in these children later in life at "confirmation." Why is this necessary, if the child had faith and knowledge from infancy? The practices of these very churches prove that they know babies do not have knowledge and faith.

And remember that 1 Corinthians 14:20 expressly states that babies are not capable of having sufficient understanding to be baptized and be members of Jesus' church.

What about repenting and confessing?

We have shown that people must repent of sin and confess Christ before baptism. And remember that the confession must be understandable so that other people know the candidate has sufficient faith to be baptized. Even if babies could have faith (which they cannot), we could never know it because they cannot understandably confess it.

And what about the responsibilities involved in church membership?

Can babies do these too? Remember, all baptized people must learn to fulfill these duties. Even if babies had faith, that would only be part of what God requires. Other things that babies cannot possibly accomplish are required, both before and after baptism.

If babies could believe, then they must also be able to DISbelieve.

But the Bible says to baptize the ones who believe and **not** the ones who do **not** believe (Mark. 16:16; Acts 8:12,36,37; etc.). Do folks who practice infant baptism distinguish the babies that believe from those that don't? If so, how? The fact is that they have no way to prove that the babies they baptize have faith; therefore, they violate Scripture by baptizing people without evidence that those people truly believe.

The Bible describes different degrees of faith (Hebrews 10:39; compare James 2:19; John 12:42,43; Matthew 14:31). Children gradually grow in understanding and in faith, but they do not have "saving" faith, sufficient to be baptized, until they are old enough to repent, confess, and fully accept the responsibility of living the Christian life, as we have already studied. Until that time they are innocent and do not need baptism.

Household Conversions

Some people refer to Bible examples where whole households were baptized. They claim that these households must have included babies, so infant baptism is authorized. But notice:

None of these examples actually say that babies were included.

Many households do not include babies or small children. If the Bible does not mention babies, then to claim there were babies in the households would simply be an unproved assumption. The fact that households were converted proves nothing by itself. Unless these passages themselves show us that babies were included, then we must settle the issue on the basis of other passages on the subject.

We have cited clear, specific evidence that people who were baptized must always first hear, believe, repent, and confess, that they must be baptized for the right reason, and that they must be able to accept the responsibilities of church membership. Babies can do none of these things. It is a misuse of Scripture to make assumptions about passages that say nothing about a subject and then use those unproved assumptions to reach conclusions that contradict the plain teaching of other Scriptures.

The contexts of the household conversions actually imply that all who were baptized did meet the conditions we have studied.

Notice each of the Bible examples of household conversions:

Cornelius's household – Acts 10:1-11:18; 15:7-11

Peter taught these people that God is no respecter of persons (10:34). So, whatever anyone in the household did to be baptized, all the rest must have done the same things. Peter did not give two sets of rules, one for babies and another for adults.

Notice some things that people in this household did that babies cannot do:

10:33,44; 11:1,14 – All came together to hear and receive what God had commanded.

10:2,35 – All in the household feared God.

15:7,9; 10:43 – They heard and believed.

11:18 – They repented.

10:35 – They were told to work righteousness.

No babies were baptized here! On the contrary, this example confirms what we have already studied: all baptized people must meet conditions that babies cannot meet.

Furthermore, God is no respecter of persons. This means we will not find any other examples of conversion in which people were baptized without meeting the conditions we have studied. Some examples may give fewer details, but no one in any household was baptized without faith, repentance, confession, etc. If such a case existed, God would be a respecter of persons.

Lydia's household – Acts 16:13-15,40

In this case there is no evidence that Lydia was even married, let alone that she had little children. The Bible teaches that the husband is the head of the household (Ephesians 5:22-25). So, whenever the Bible describes households in which the man of the house is involved, if anybody is mentioned by name then the man is mentioned. (Notice how the other household conversions demonstrate this.)

Since no man is mentioned when Lydia's household was baptized, this implies that there was no man to be the head of the household. Her household may have included relatives, especially older relatives, and perhaps servants, but no husband is implied, let alone children.

Paul later "encouraged" those who were brethren (NKJV), including Lydia's house (verse 40). Did this include babies?

The Jailer's household – Acts 16:23-34

Before this household was baptized, Paul spoke the word to all in the house (verse 32), and they believed (verses 31,34). Again, babies can't do these things, so no babies were included among those baptized here.

Stephanas' household – 1 Corinthians 1:16; 16:15

Again, what verse says there were babies in this household? Note that Stephanas' house ministered to the saints. Again, the people who were baptized were old enough to be active in God's work as members of the church. This does not include babies.

The household conversions do not disprove what we have learned elsewhere. Instead they harmonize with it. All who are baptized must do things that babies cannot do. Therefore, the command to be baptized does not include babies. When people baptize babies, they follow human authority, and they displease God.

Titus 1:10,11 – Whole houses can be "overthrown" or subverted.

If household conversions prove babies can be baptized, then household subversions prove babies can apostatize. And if babies have been subverted, then we should not baptize them. So, again, how do we know which should be baptized and which should not?

Conclusion

Infant baptism is objectionable for several reasons.

First, infant baptism is an unauthorized change in God's pattern for baptism.

God tells us whom to baptize. He tells the conditions people must meet before, during, and after baptism; but babies do not fit. To baptize babies is to act by human authority without divine authority.

Second, infant baptism leads people to believe they are saved when they are not.

God requires people to be baptized for the remission of sins when they are old enough to make their own decisions with true understanding, etc. But people, who have been baptized as babies, later become old enough to be responsible for their conduct. At that point, they should be baptized, but they often refuse because they believe they have already been baptized

Their infant baptism was not Scriptural, but it leads them to refuse Scriptural baptism. The result is that many people go through their whole lives never having been Scripturally baptized, and therefore never receiving forgiveness of sins!

A final objection to infant baptism is that it is almost always done by sprinkling or pouring, not by immersion.

But the Bible says that baptism is a burial (Romans 6:4; Colossians 2:12). A person must go down into the water and come up out of it (Acts 8:38,39; Mark 1:9,10). Bible baptism requires washing the whole body in water (Hebrews 10:23). The Bible evidence shows that baptism must be an immersion, not a sprinkling or pouring. Infant baptism does not fit God's pattern on any of these points.

What should a person do if his baptism was not done the way the Bible teaches? He should realize that he simply has not yet obeyed God, and he needs to obey God by being baptized according to the Bible (see Acts 19:1-6). If this is your need, we urge you to find a faithful local church belonging to Christ and be baptized Scripturally today!

The Purpose of Baptism

Introduction:

Baptism is important.

Matthew 28:18-20 records the "Great Commission." Jesus here commands all people, in becoming His disciples, to be taught His word and be baptized. This account shows baptism is important:

(1) Baptism is based on Jesus' own authority. He has commanded it. Anything He commands is important and must be taught and practiced as He commanded it to be. Men have no right to change what Jesus has instituted.

(Matthew 15:9,13; Galatians 1:8,9; 2 John 9-11; Colossians 3:17; Jeremiah 10:23; Proverbs 14:12; 3:5,6; Revelation 22:18,19)

(2) It is a fundamental part of becoming a disciple.

(3) Jesus wants everyone in the world to be taught about it.

Everyone needs to understand Jesus' teaching about baptism and practice it the way He said to do it.

Yet baptism is highly controversial and often misunderstood.

Important as baptism is, many people are confused about it. Some admit they do not understand it. Others claim to understand it, but their practice differs from what Jesus taught.

Without question, people need to study baptism to be sure they have obeyed Jesus' will.

The purpose of this lesson is to study the purpose of baptism.

Why should a person be baptized in water? What goal should he intend his baptism to accomplish?

Different Views of the Purpose of Baptism

Two Views of the Purpose of Baptism

One view is that baptism is a sign that a person has already been forgiven.

Consider a lost sinner who has never received forgiveness by Jesus' blood and never become a Christian. Some churches say that such a person must believe in Jesus, then at that point Jesus forgives his sins (some add that he must repent of sins and confess Jesus or pray for forgiveness).

This view means that baptism is not essential to receive forgiveness, but one should be baptized **after** he has been forgiven. The purpose of baptism, they say, is to provide an outward sign to show others that he has been saved, or perhaps to join a particular denomination.

> "Baptism is not essential to salvation ... but it is essential to obedience, since Christ commanded it. It is also essential to membership in the church which is his body." – *Standard Manual for Baptist Churches*, Hiscox (pp. 20,21)

> "Is baptism necessary for salvation? I don't beat about the bush about it at all. I come out with a plain, definite, NO! No, baptism doesn't save, doesn't help save, and I'll go even further to say that it doesn't have anything in this world to do with the saving of a soul." – *Good News*, 3/2/72 (a Baptist paper)

> The Seventh Day Adventist "Baptismal Vow" requires a person, *before* baptism, to answer this question: "...have you accepted Jesus Christ as your personal Savior, and do you believe that God, for Christ's sake, has forgiven your sins, and given you a new heart.

This is standard doctrine in Protestant churches, though some emphasize it more than others. So, when a person expresses a desire for baptism, most churches schedule him/her for a baptismal service at some future date. They believe the person is saved in the meanwhile, so there is no hurry.

(All above quotations are taken from the *Handbook of Religious Quotations*.)

The other view is that one must be baptized in order to receive remission of sins.

This view teaches that one must truly believe in Jesus, repent, and confess Christ. It emphasizes that the blood of Jesus is what forgives a person's sins. But it also teaches that sins are not forgiven until the person has been baptized.

This means that the purpose of baptism is to receive forgiveness. To be a Scriptural baptism, it must be done for the purpose of being cleansed or freed from sins by the blood of Jesus. So, a person stands justified before God only after he has been baptized, not before.

Why Does the Question Matter?

Either way the person is baptized, so why does it matter what his purpose is?

Acts of service to God must be done from proper motives.

Romans 6:17,18 – To be made free from sin, we must obey God from the **heart**. Service to God is not acceptable if we just go through outward motions. We must understand and sincerely mean what we do. This principle can be illustrated by other works of service to God.

1 Corinthians 14:15 – Singing and prayer must be done with the spirit and the understanding. Outward actions are not enough.

1 Corinthians 11:26-29 – In the Lord's supper we must recognize the spiritual meaning of the elements. If we do not discern the Lord's body, we eat and drink damnation to our souls.

God requires proper outward actions, but He also requires proper motives and purposes.

(1 Corinthians 13:1-3; Psalm 51:6,10; Proverbs 4:23)

When God assigns a purpose to an act, the purpose becomes part of the pattern.

Galatians 1:8 – Our service to God must conform to His word, without changing the pattern. When God reveals the purpose for an act, if we do it for a different purpose, we have changed the pattern.

2 John 9 – One who does not abide in Jesus' teaching does not have the Father and Son. So whatever Jesus' word teaches about the purpose of baptism, we must abide in that teaching. If we practice a different purpose, we have gone beyond what Jesus revealed.

Acts 19:1-5 – Here Paul found some men who had been baptized by immersion in water. If the outward act is all that matters, their baptism would have been fine. But they had to be baptized again to do it right, so clearly there was something wrong with their understanding of the purpose. The same would be true of anyone today whose baptism did not fit the gospel pattern.

When we teach the importance of baptism, people sometimes accuse us of over-emphasizing outward actions. The opposite is true. The reason we emphasize baptism is that inner intentions and purposes do matter. When people say baptism is not necessary so we can overlook the purpose for baptism, they are the ones who are teaching that the meaning does not matter.

(Matthew 15:9,13; Colossians 3:17; Jeremiah 10:23; Proverbs 14:12; 3:5,6; Revelation 22:18,19)

Scriptures about the Purpose of Baptism

We will consider six fundamental passages (though there are others that teach the same).

Mark 16:15,16 - He Who Believes and Is Baptized Will Be Saved.

Where does this passage place salvation in relation to baptism?

Does salvation come before baptism or as a result of it? We can no more be saved before baptism than we can before believing.

It is like 1 + 1 = 2. Take away either of the "1's" and you no longer have two. Likewise, if you take away either faith or baptism, you no longer have salvation.

Some respond: "It says you will be condemned if you don't believe, but it doesn't say you will be condemned if you are not baptized."

The Bible does not always spell out what we have to do to be lost. It tells us what we have to do to be saved and expects us to realize, if we don't do that, we will be lost.

According to Luke 7:30, when people refuse baptism, they reject the counsel of God. So Jesus had already taught that those who refuse to be baptized have rejected God's word.

But in Mark 16:16, Jesus said we must do **two** things to be **saved**. To be lost, you only need to omit one or the other of them. The person who does not have faith probably would not be baptized, and it would not do any good if he did. To be lost is easy – just don't believe. To be saved is harder – you must both believe and be baptized.

Further, Jesus said to believe the **gospel** (verses 15,16). What does the gospel say? It says, "He who believes and is baptized will be saved." That is what the **gospel** teaches, so that is what people who seek salvation must **believe**. What if I don't believe that? Then I don't believe the gospel! What does the passage say about people who don't believe the gospel?

Note the difference between what men say and what Jesus said:

Men say: He who believes is saved and may then be baptized.

Jesus said: He who believes and is baptized will be saved. Both faith and baptism are essential in order to receive salvation.

Remember, we cannot please God by following human doctrines that differ from the gospel (Galatians 1:8; Matthew 15:9; etc.).

Acts 2:38 - Repent and Be Baptized for Remission of Sins.

Where does this passage place remission in relation to baptism?

Are sins forgiven (remitted) before baptism or as a result of it? Note that the **purpose** of baptism is clearly stated: it is **for remission** of sins.

What does "for remission of sins" mean?

Some say that "for" means "because of," like "He received a ticket for speeding" – i.e., because he had been speeding (not in order that he might speed). "For" can have this meaning in English, but the word cannot mean this in Acts 2:38.

The ASV says, "unto the remission of your sins." The NRSV says, "so that your sins may be forgiven." The Modern Literal Version currently translates "into the forgiveness of your sins," and the footnote says regarding the translation "for":

> ... not everyone is ever satisfied. But they only complain about Acts 2:38 not the other four places this same Greek construction is in the Bible. ... 'For' in English can mean 'because' but this word is 'eis' ... No translation has ever used 'because' or 'because of' in Acts 2:38, including the ones made by the Baptist denomination ...

Consider the people to whom Peter was speaking.

If "for" means because they already had remission, then Peter must have been talking to people who were already saved. But was he?

He had just convicted them of killing Jesus (verse 36), and they were pricked in heart and asked what to do (verse 37). They did not already have remission, but stood in need of receiving it.

Peter then told them to "repent." If they already had remission, why did they need to repent? The command to repent proves these people were not saved but were sinners who needed to receive remission.

Peter also told them to "be saved" from that wicked generation (verse 40). If they had already been forgiven, why did he tell them to be saved?

Surely these were not saved people being told what to do because they already **had** remission. They were lost sinners being told what to do in order to **receive** remission. So, "for remission of sins" in verse 38 means to be baptized "in order to receive remission."

Consider the parallel to Matthew 26:28.

Matthew 26:28 says Jesus' **blood** would be shed for many "***for*** remission of sins."

Acts 2:38 says be **baptized** "***for*** remission of sins."

Did Jesus shed His blood because people already had remission of sins? No, He shed His blood so people who did not have remission could **receive** it.

Likewise, baptism is administered, not because people already have remission, but so people who do not have it can receive it.

Suppose a person was baptized without understanding that the gospel says he should be baptized in order to receive remission of sins. Suppose he believed he was saved before baptism. Then would he be baptized in order to receive remission? How could he if he believed he already had salvation? How then could his baptism harmonize with the pattern of God's word?

1 Peter 3:21 - Baptism Saves Us.

Noah illustrates how we are saved. Verse 20 says he and his family were saved "by (or through) water." The flood water destroyed wicked people; but it also saved Noah because it bore the ark up, delivering (saving) Noah from death.

This illustrates the fact that what saves us is baptism. This does not refer to physically washing dirt from our bodies. The power is not in the water but in the death and resurrection of Jesus. But baptism is the point at which we contact Jesus' blood so we are saved.

Galatians 3:27 - We Are Baptized into Jesus.

How many people are in Christ? Just as many as **have been baptized** into Him. What if a person has not been baptized into Christ? Then that person is not in Him.

Why is it important to be in Christ?
* Ephesians 1:7 – Forgiveness of sins is in Christ.
* 2 Timothy 2:10 – Salvation is in Him.
* 1 John 5:11,12 – Eternal life is in the Son
* Ephesians 1:3 – All spiritual blessings are in Christ.

(Compare Romans 8:1; 2 Corinthians 5:17; Philippians 4:7.)

If a person is outside Christ, he does not have forgiveness, salvation, eternal life, or the other spiritual blessings that are in Christ. But how does one come into Christ? He must be baptized into Christ. Then what is the condition of one who has not been baptized or who does not believe baptism is for the purpose of being saved?

Hearing, believing, repenting, and confession are all essential steps toward Christ, but baptism is the step that puts a person **into** Christ. Before baptism, a person is still outside Christ, still without forgiveness and the other blessings that are in Christ. If he wants those blessings, he must be baptized for the purpose of coming into Christ.

Romans 6:3 - We Are Baptized into Jesus' Death.

Like Galatians 3:27, this verse says we are **baptized** into Jesus. But it also says we are baptized into Jesus' **death**.

Why is Jesus' death important to us? It was in His death that He shed His blood that saves us from sin! How do we come into contact with His saving death? We are baptized into it!

When we teach that baptism is necessary to salvation, often we are accused of not believing in salvation by Jesus' blood. The truth is just the opposite. The reason we believe baptism is necessary is that baptism is where the sinner contacts Jesus' blood! Those who say you are saved **before** baptism are (unintentionally) saying you are saved without Jesus' blood, because they are teaching the sinner is saved before he contacts the blood!

In baptism we receive the benefits of Jesus' death! What then is the condition of those who say you are saved before baptism or that baptism is not necessary for the remission of sins?

Acts 22:16 - Be Baptized and Wash away Your Sins.

Where is the washing away of sins in this passage: before baptism or a result that follows from baptism?

Before he was baptized, the sinner in this story (Saul) had already done everything most churches say one must do to be saved.

He had seen Jesus on the road, he clearly believed in Him, and he was willing to obey Him (22:5-10; 9:3-6). He had even been praying (9:9,11). If anyone could be saved before baptism, it would have been Saul. But was he saved?

Jesus had said Saul should go into the city and be **told** what he **must** do (9:6). Ananias came and **told** him to be **baptized** and **wash away his sins**.

If sins are forgiven before baptism, Saul would have had no sins to wash away when Ananias arrived. But he still had his sins till he was baptized. So today, though a person may believe in Jesus and repent, he is still guilty of all his sins till he is baptized.

That is why in Bible examples of conversion, people never postponed baptism.

Always, as soon as the sinner understood the Bible teaching, believed, and repented, he was baptized immediately:

Acts 2:41 – "That day" 3000 were baptized.

Acts 8:36 – "What hinders me from being baptized?"
Acts 9:18 – "Immediately ... he arose and was baptized"
Acts 16:33 – "...the same hour of the night ... immediately he and all his family were baptized"
Acts 22:16 – "...why are you waiting? Arise and be baptized, and wash away your sins...."

When modern denominations postpone the baptism of penitent believers to some future baptismal service, they are not following the Bible pattern regarding the urgency of baptism. The reason they postpone baptism is that they do not believe the proper purpose of baptism. They believe the person is already saved, so what's the hurry?

When we understand that a person is still in sin until he is baptized, then we understand why people in the Bible did not postpone baptism.

Conclusion

According to the passages we have studied, the purpose of baptism is as follows:

Mark 16:16 – Baptism is required in order to be saved.
Acts 2:38 – Baptism is for (in order to receive) remission of sins.
1 Peter 3:21 – Baptism saves us.
Galatians 3:27 – We are baptized into Christ.
Romans 6:3 – We are baptized into Jesus' death.
Acts 22:16 – Baptism is necessary for sins to be washed away.

These are all different ways of saying the same thing. To teach that one is saved before baptism is to teach a human gospel different from what the Lord authorized. Those who are baptized according to such a doctrine have not received a Scriptural baptism.

What should such people do? Like the men in Acts 19:1-6, they should be baptized in harmony with the teaching of the gospel. Then they receive forgiveness by the blood of Jesus.

What about you? Have you been baptized properly? Are you living a faithful life?

Should a Person Who Is Not a Child of God Pray for Forgiveness?

Introduction:

One of the most important questions anyone can ask is, "What must I do to be saved?" If a person is not a child of God, having never been born again, yet wants to be forgiven of sins, what must such a person do?

Many churches teach that such a person should simply believe on Jesus and then <u>pray for forgiveness</u>.

Consider the following quotation from a tract entitled "God's Simple Plan of Salvation."

> "Simply believe on Him as the one who bore **your sin, died** in **your place**, was buried and was raised for **your justification**. Now call upon Him. 'For whosoever shall call upon the name of the Lord, shall be saved' (Romans 10:13). The first prayer for a sinner to pray is given in Luke 18:13: 'God be merciful **to me a sinner**.' Now you are a sinner and surely you are sorry because of it. Right **now**, wherever you are, lift your heart to God in prayer ... Just say: O, God, I am a sinner. I am sorry, I repent, have **mercy** upon me, and **save** me for Jesus' sake. Now just take **Him** at His word ... You say, 'surely that is not all that is necessary to do to be saved.' Yes it is, absolutely all ... **After you are saved ... [t]hen you should be baptized**..." [All emphasis in the original.]

The purpose of this study is to consider what the Bible says about this doctrine.

The gospel reveals many examples in which people who were not children of God were converted. In which of these examples was anyone ever told to pray to receive forgiveness? And where does the Bible say that a person is saved before he is baptized, then **after** he is saved he should be baptized?

These are serious questions because they pertain to whether or not a person is forgiven of sin. We cannot be saved if we follow a pattern of salvation that differs from what God reveals in the gospel. Anyone who preaches a different gospel is accursed (Galatians 1:8,9). Following man-made doctrines makes our service to God vain (Matthew 15:9,14).

So should a person who is not a child of God pray for forgiveness? Is this doctrine in the gospel or was it invented by men?

Does the Gospel Teach People Who Are Not Children of God to Pray for Forgiveness?

Consider what the gospel says about prayer.

Who Has the Right to Pray to God?

Whose prayer will God hear?

1 John 3:22 – We receive what we pray for if we **keep God's commands** and do what pleases Him.

James 5:16 – The prayer of a **righteous** man avails much.

Proverbs 15:8,29 – God hears and delights in the prayer of the **righteous**, but He is far from the wicked. If one turns his ear away from the law, his prayer is an abomination to God. (28:9)

John 9:31 – God hears not sinners, but does hear those who **worship and obey Him**.

So God hears the prayers of obedient righteous people. But we are studying about disobedient, unrighteous people. What about their prayers? These verses say that God refuses to hear their prayers. We will later consider the case of a man who was diligently seeking truth. But in general God does not even hear the prayers of those who are not His children.

(See also Psalm 34:15,16; 1 Peter 3:12.)

Who Can Pray for Forgiveness?

There are, however, examples of people who did pray for forgiveness. Who were these people?

Matthew 6:12 – Jesus said to pray, "Forgive us our debts (trespasses)."

But who was taught to pray this prayer? Jesus was speaking to Jews, children of Israel (4:25). These were children of God under the Old Testament (remember, Jesus' gospel did not take effect till He died – Hebrews 9:16,17; Colossians 2:14).

These people were also Jesus' disciples (5:1,2). They were able to address God as "Our Father," so they were children of God (6:9). The instruction to pray for forgiveness was never given to those who were **not** children of God but only to those who were **already** children of God.

Luke 18:13,14 – The publican prayed, "God be merciful to me, a sinner," and he was justified.

The tract we quoted earlier used this to prove one who is not a child of God should pray for forgiveness. But was this man a child of God or not?

Notice that both the publican and the Pharisee went up to the **Temple** to pray (18:10). But this was the Jewish temple, and only Jews in covenant relationship with God were allowed to enter (Acts 21:28). So, the publican was a Jew just like the Pharisee was: a child of God under the Old Testament. This passage tells us nothing about what should be done by a person who is **not** a child of child of God.

Furthermore, remember that all this occurred while the Old Testament was still binding. In that Jewish Temple, Levitical priests still offered animal sacrifices to atone for sin. Surely this case does not describe God's way of forgiving lost sinners under the New Testament. The New Testament system of justification was not yet even in effect.

Acts 8:13-22 – Simon sinned and was told to repent and pray for forgiveness.

Was Simon a child of God or not? 8:12 says the Samaritans believed the gospel and were baptized. This is exactly what Mark 16:16 says to do to be saved, so the Samaritans were saved.

8:13 says Simon "**also**" believed and was baptized. He did just what the other Samaritans did. If they were saved, then so was he.

But **after** he was forgiven, Simon sinned again and was told to repent and pray for forgiveness (8:18-22). So again, a child of God who sins should pray for forgiveness, but nowhere does this teach one who is **not** a child of God to pray for forgiveness.

1 John 1:8-10 – If we "confess our sins," God will forgive us.

But who are the "we" who are here told to confess sins? 1:7 says that "we" are those who walk in the light, have fellowship with God, being cleansed by His blood. 2:1-6 says "we" are those who know God (verse 3) and are in Him (verses 5,6), in contrast to the world (verse 2).

If any doubt remains, 3:2 plainly says "*we are children of God.*" The whole context refers to children of God.

All these verses show that, under the gospel, children of God sometimes sin. They are told to repent and pray for forgiveness. But passages that talk about praying for forgiveness are always talking about children of God. *There is not one passage or example anywhere in the gospel that tells people who are not children of God to pray for forgiveness.* That doctrine is a doctrine of men (Matthew 15:9).

What Should a Person Who Is Not a Child of God Do to Be Forgiven?

If such people are not told to pray for forgiveness, then what should they do? In particular, does the Bible teach (as the tract said) that people are saved before baptism, then they are baptized after they are saved? Consider some New Testament examples of conversion.

The Jews on Pentecost - Acts 2

These people were the same ones who were responsible for Jesus' death. Verse 21 says they were told, "Whosoever shall call on the name of the Lord shall be saved" (compare Romans 10:13). This is a statement the tract used to prove non-Christians should pray for forgiveness.

But what does it mean to "call on the name of the Lord"? How does one do this? The statement does not really say to *pray* to God. Keep the verse in context and the Bible will explain itself. The sermon isn't over yet!

As Peter preached, the people recognized their sins and asked what they should do (verse 37). Here is the question we need answered. What should alien sinners do to be forgiven?

Peter said, "*Repent and be baptized ... for remission of sins...*" (verse 38). This tells how the people were saved. Peter had said to call on the name of the Lord, but when asked specifically what should be done, he said to repent and be baptized for remission of sins.

Some people say "for remission of sins" means "because they had the remission of sins," like "He was given a ticket for speeding," or "He was paid for working." So they say people should pray for forgiveness, then God forgives them, then they are baptized because they have been forgiven.

But if that is so, then these people must have been saved **before** verse 38, and verse 38 tells them how to show they have already been saved. But if that is the case, why did Peter in verse 38 tell them to

Salvation through Jesus Christ

repent? Do people who have just been cleansed of their sins need to repent? No, clearly Peter was talking to people who were still guilty of their sins, telling them how to be forgiven. So, "for remission of sins" does not mean "because you have remission." Rather, it means "in order that you may receive remission," just like it means in Matthew 26:28.

So Acts 2:21 says to call on the Lord's name but does not tell how to do so. When people say this refers to prayer, they are assuming what they must prove. The information about how to call on the Lord to receive remission of sins is given in verse 38. It says every lost sinner must repent and be baptized for remission of sins. This is what a person who is not a child of God must do to be forgiven.

Cornelius - Acts 10 & 11

Acts 10:1,2 says Cornelius was a generous, religious man who "prayed to God." Verses 4,5,31 say God "heard" his prayer, and His prayers were a memorial to God. At this point Cornelius was not a child of God. Yet because he was seeking God's will, God knew He was praying. The passage does not say what Cornelius was praying for, but we will see that it does tell us what he received!

But our main question is this: Was Cornelius ***forgiven*** when he prayed to God? Acts 11:14 says an angel told him to send for Peter, who would tell him ***words*** whereby he could be saved. When Peter arrived, did he tell Cornelius to pray for forgiveness? No, he told him to be ***baptized*** in water (10:47,48).

If a person who is not a child of God is saved by praying, why wasn't Cornelius saved before Peter spoke to him? He had surely been praying, yet the passage clearly says that he had to hear words whereby he could be ***saved***. Then the words that he heard told him to be ***baptized***.

The only thing the New Testament says God has ever given an alien sinner in response to prayer is an opportunity to hear the gospel. Neither Cornelius nor any other alien sinner was ever told to pray for forgiveness, nor did such people ever receive forgiveness by praying. What Cornelius needed in order to be saved was baptism. And that is what every alien sinner today needs.

Saul of Tarsus - Acts 9 & 22

Saul had been persecuting Jesus' church, but Jesus appeared to him on the road to Damascus and told him to go into the city where he would be told what he ***must do*** (9:1-6). In the city, he fasted and prayed (9:9,11). Note that no one ever told him to pray. He was to be ***told*** what he must do, but he was praying ***before*** he was told what to do!

But was he ***forgiven*** by praying? If believing and praying are "absolutely all" one must do to be forgiven, then surely Saul was forgiven **before** he was told what he must do! But does the Bible say he was saved then?

In Acts 9:18 Ananias came to tell Saul what he **must do**, and as a result Saul was immediately **baptized**. Acts 22:16 explains why he did this, because it records what Ananias told Saul to do. Ananias said, "And now why are you waiting? Arise and be baptized, and wash away your sins, calling on the name of the Lord."

Note the following important lessons here:

(1) Saul was to be **told** what he must do, but he was never told to pray for forgiveness.

(2) Even though Saul did pray, yet he was not forgiven by prayer, for he still needed to have his sins washed away. If a non-Christian today prays for forgiveness, he will still be exactly like Saul: he will still be in his sins!

(3) When Ananias arrived, Saul had been **praying:** the very thing denominational preachers tell non-Christians to do. But Ananias said, "And now why are you **waiting**?" In effect he told Saul to **stop** what he had been doing and do something else instead!

(4) When Ananias told Saul what he "must do," he said to be **baptized** and wash away his sins, calling on the name of the Lord. That confirms what we learned in Acts 2. How does a person who is not a child of God call on the name of the Lord? Not by prayer, but in **baptism**!

(5) This also confirms that sins are not forgiven **before** baptism, but baptism is a necessary condition in order to have sins washed away by Jesus' blood. This agrees with what is taught in many other Scriptures, such as Mark 16:16; Romans 6:3,4; Galatians 3:27; and 1 Peter 3:21.

When alien sinners have been taught to pray for forgiveness, they need to understand what Saul was told. They need to realize that they will not be forgiven by praying, but what they need to do is to be **baptized** for remission of sins!

Conclusion

Consider a brief summary of what we have learned:

* Generally, God does not hear the prayers of people who are not His children.

* The only people in the New Testament who received forgiveness as a result of prayer were people who were already children of God but had sinned again.

* No one, who was not a child of God, was ever told by any inspired man to pray for forgiveness of sins. That doctrine is therefore a man-made doctrine.

* When such people for some reason did pray to God, they did not receive forgiveness as a result.

* In all cases, people who were not children of God had to be **baptized** in order to receive forgiveness of sins. In no case did any person ever receive forgiveness of sins before he was baptized.

Matthew 7:21-23 teaches that it is not enough simply to **call** Jesus our Lord and sincerely think we are serving Him. We must **do** the will of the Father in heaven. True calling on the Lord is not accomplished simply by what we **say**, but by what we **do**!

The Father's will is that a person who is not a child of God needs to believe, repent, confess Christ (Romans 10:9,10), and be baptized for remission of sins. Preachers who teach such people to pray for forgiveness have **changed** God's plan. ***They have substituted prayer for baptism!*** Any church and any preacher who teaches such a doctrine is preaching a different gospel from what the inspired apostles preached. Note Galatians 1:8,9.

Now suppose a person believed he was saved as a result of prayer, and then he was baptized thinking he was saved before the baptism. What should such a person do? Despite his sincerity, he has never been baptized for the Scriptural reason, so his baptism did not achieve the purpose for which it was intended. But the purpose of baptism is to wash away sins by the blood of Jesus. If a person has not done this properly, then he has never been forgiven of his sins at all! To please God, he needs to be baptized Scripturally, like the men did in Acts 19:1-5.

Are You Really "Born Again"?

Introduction:

Many sincere religious people often speak about "born-again Christians," "born-again believers," etc. In this study, let us consider exactly how a person is "born again."

How does a person know whether he has been born again? Is it possible to think we have been born again when we really have not been? Some will reply that, to be born again you must accept Jesus as your personal Savior. But how does this happen? What does the Bible say?

How Important Are Hearing and Believing?

Hearing the Gospel

1 Peter 1:22-25 – *We are "born again" by the incorruptible seed, which is God's word (verse 23), the gospel (verse 25).*

When a person is born physically, he becomes a child in a family. When one is born again, he becomes a spiritual child of God, a member of God's family. This process is similar to the reproduction of plants or animals. Birth is the product of **seed** that is planted, germinates, and produces a new organism.

Spiritually, the seed by which we become children of God is God's word (compare Luke 8:11). This is planted in men's hearts when they hear the gospel. If they then believe and obey the gospel, they become "born again" as Christians. (Compare James 1:18; 1 Corinthians 4:15.)

Galatians 6:7 – But seed reproduces after its kind. "Whatever a man sows…"

So, one must be sure that the seed (message) he hears and believes is really the true gospel. If one plants the wrong seed in his garden, he will not grow the kind of plant he wants. And if one accepts some spiritual message that is different from the gospel, he would not really be born again, even though he might think he had been.

Believing the Gospel

John 1:12 – To have the power or right to become a child of God ("born again"), one must believe in Jesus.

A popular tract entitled "Have You Been Born Again?" says, "The moment a lost sinner repents of his sins and trusts Jesus as the only One who can save Him (sic), he is born again." But note that this differs from John 1:12: The Scripture does not say that believing immediately makes one a child of God. It says that believing gives one **the right or power to become** a child of God.

I once bought a ticket to a football game, but the weather turned out so bad I decided not to go. The ticket gave me the **power** to attend, but did not automatically make me a spectator. Other things also had to happen.

We often receive letters saying we have been approved for charge cards. Approval gives us the power to get the card, but that does not mean we automatically have the card. Other things have to happen.

So faith gives you the power to become a child of God, but by itself it does not automatically and immediately make you a child of God. Other things still have to happen afterward.

John 1:13 – We can be born again only by following God's will, not man's will.

Remember, God's word is the seed that makes children of God. Other seeds, especially man-made doctrines, do not have the power to save.

It follows that the only way you or I can be sure we are born again is by knowing what the word of God says. If a person was taught and followed doctrine that differs from God's word, he would not be truly born again, no matter what he may think about it.

Note Galatians 1:8,9; Matthew 15:9,13; 7:21-23; 2 John 9-11; Jeremiah 10:23; Proverbs 14:12; 3:5,6.

Other Passages about Hearing and Believing the Gospel

Other passages confirm that hearing and believing are necessary to salvation.

John 6:44,45 – You cannot come to Jesus without hearing, learning, and being taught God's word.

John 8:31,32,24 – To be made free from sin, you must know the truth and believe in Jesus.

Romans 1:16 – The gospel is the power of God to save those who believe.

Romans 10:17 – Faith comes by hearing God's word.

What about you? Do you believe you have been born again? The only way to know is if the Scriptures say to do what you did. Can you find passages that say you can be born again by doing what you did? Have you considered all that God's word says on the subject?

(John 6:63; Hebrews 11:6; John 3:3-7; Galatians 3:26,27)

How Important Is Obedience, Including Baptism?

We have learned that believing, though essential, only gives the right to **become** a child of God. What else is needed?

We earlier quoted a common doctrine that a person is born again the moment he believes, so there is nothing more to do. In particular, many folks believe that baptism is important but is not essential in order to become a saved child of God. What does the Bible say?

How Important Is Obedience?

1 Peter 1:22-25 said we are born again by God's word. But verse 22 adds that we must **obey the truth** in order to purify our souls. We are born again by the word only when we **do** what it instructs us to do!

Many other scriptures confirm that obedience is necessary in order to receive forgiveness by Jesus' blood. Note a few of them:

Romans 6:17,18 – We are made free from sin as a result of **obeying** the doctrine delivered from God.

Hebrews 5:9 – Jesus is the author of eternal salvation to all who **obey** Him.

2 Thessalonians 1:8,9 – Those who **do not obey** the gospel will be punished with everlasting destruction.

Matthew 7:21-23 – Some who believed in Jesus will yet be condemned because they did not **do** the will of the Father.

So obedience is necessary, in addition to faith, in order to be born again.

How Important Is Baptism?

Notice now in particular whether or not baptism is required to become a child of God.

2 Corinthians 5:17 – If anyone is in Christ, he is a new creation.

"New creation" is another way of saying "born again" (we will confirm this as we proceed). To be a new creation, one must be "in Christ": in fellowship and harmony with Christ. Surely no one can be born again if he is still outside Christ.

(Note also 2 Timothy 2:10; Ephesians 1:7; 1 John 5:11,12; Romans 8:1.)

So to be born again, we need to know how to come "into Christ." What does the Bible say?

Romans 6:3,4 – We are "baptized into Christ."

If so, how could anyone be in Christ without baptism or before baptism? And since we must be in Christ to be born again, how could one be born again without or before baptism? That would be like saying a person who is **outside** a house can be **inside** the house without ever coming **into** it.

Further, the passage says we are baptized "into Jesus' **death**." But His death is what saves and forgives us so we can be children of God. Verses 6 & 7 then add that, when we have been baptized (verses 3,4), the body of sin is done away and we are free from sin (verses 17,18).

Verse 4 clinches the conclusion by saying that, as a result of being buried in baptism and rising from it, we have "**newness of life**": we are born again! This does not in any way belittle the need for faith, repentance, and confession. But essential as those are, they are not enough without baptism.

Baptism is essential in order to come into Christ, into His death, and to have newness of life. Clearly a person must be baptized in order to be born again.

Galatians 3:26,27 – As many as are baptized into Christ, have put Christ on.

How many are "in Christ"? As many as have been **baptized** into Him: no more and no less. But remember we are born again only when we are in Christ. So how many are born again? As many as have been Scripturally baptized: no more and no less.

This connection is confirmed by verse 26. Note the verb tenses:

"For you **are** all sons of God through faith in Christ Jesus. For as many of you as **were** baptized into Christ have put on Christ." Notice:

This	must come	This
You **were** baptized into Christ	**before**	You **are** sons of God.

This must happen "by faith" because, as we learned earlier, faith gives one the right or power to become a child of God. One who lacks faith has no right to be baptized (Mark 16:15,16; Acts 8:35-39). But *after* faith has led to **baptism**, only then is one a child of God (born again).

Other passages also confirm that baptism is necessary in order to be forgiven by Jesus' blood:

Mark 16:15,16 – To be saved, one must believe **and** be baptized.

Acts 2:38 – Everyone must repent and be baptized for the forgiveness of sins.

Acts 22:16 – Saul had believed in Jesus, but he was told to be baptized and wash away his sins.

1 Peter 3:21 – Baptism also now saves us. This occurs, not by the power of water, but by the power of Jesus as manifested in the resurrection. Nevertheless, baptism is necessary to receive that power.

If people in sin want to be born again, they must believe in Jesus enough to repent of sin, confess Christ, and be baptized for the forgiveness of sins.

A Summary Passage – John 3:3-7

Let us summarize what we have learned so far:

1. Hearing then believing gives one the **right** to become a child of God (John 1:12).
2. But to be born again one must **obey** the gospel (1 Peter 1:22-25).
3. One is born again only when he is **in Christ** (2 Corinthians 5:17).
4. But to come into Christ, he must be **baptized** (Romans 6:3,4; Galatians 3:26,27).

With this background, let us examine the best-known text about the new birth – John 3:3-7. Verse 3 says that, to enter the kingdom, one must be born again. Verse 5 says one must be born of the water and the Spirit. So this new birth involves two elements: the "water" and the "Spirit." Let us examine each.

To What Does the "Water" Refer?

Some say that "water" in John 3:5 refers to physical birth.

But consider the following facts:

(1) There is no **evidence** whatever that water here refers to physical birth. It is simply speculation.

(2) The gospel never uses the word "water" to refer to physical birth.

(3) John 3 mentions physical birth; but it was suggested, not by Jesus, but by Nicodemus because he was confused and misunderstood Jesus' teaching. Jesus rebuked Nicodemus for this and then **contrasted** physical birth and the new birth, showing they are **different** (verse 6). That means that, when people think the "water" refers to physical birth, they misunderstand just like Nicodemus did!

(4) Comparing verse 3 to verse 5 shows that being "born of water and of the Spirit" (verse 5) is just another way of saying "be born again" (verse 3). Verse 5 just clarifies and explains verse 3.

| "born again" (verse 3) = "born of water and the Spirit" (verse 5) |

So, the "water" of verse 5 is **part** of the new birth. It does not refer to some **other** birth.

"Water" in John 3:5 must refer to water baptism.

Baptism fits perfectly because:

(1) Baptism is the only command in the New Testament that **requires** the use of "water" (Acts 8:35-39; 10:47; John 3:23; Hebrews 10:22; etc.). So, in the gospel "water" never refers to physical birth, but it often refers to baptism.

(2) As shown previously, many other passages teach that water baptism is essential to salvation.

(3) In particular, we have shown several passages that expressly include baptism as an essential element of the new birth.

(4) We will see that many passages tie baptism to the hearing of the gospel, exactly like John 3:5 does.

John 3:5 simply confirms our previous conclusion that water baptism is necessary to the new birth.

To What Does the "Spirit" Refer?

The "Spirit" can also be understood from what we have already studied.

We have already learned that, before baptism, one must hear and believe the **word,** which is the seed by which we are born again (1 Peter 1:23). But the Holy Spirit revealed the word so people might learn it and be saved (2 Peter 1:21; Ephesians 3:3-5; John 14:26; 16:13; 1 Corinthians 2:10-13).

Ephesians 6:17 – The word is the "sword of the Spirit." It is the tool or means the Spirit uses to accomplish His work in conversion.

So, one is "born of water and the Spirit" when one learns and believes the **gospel message**, as revealed by the **Spirit**, and then obeys that message by being **baptized**.

Other passages likewise tie the word of the Spirit to baptism in conversion.

Note some parallels:
John 3:5 – Be born of **water** and the **Spirit**.
Mark 16:15,16 – Preach the **gospel**. He who believes and is **baptized** will be saved.
Acts 2:41 – Those who gladly received the **word** were **baptized**.
Acts 8:12 – People who believed the **gospel** were **baptized**.
Acts 8:35-39; 16:32,33; 18:8 – Other examples in which the word was preached and people were baptized.
Ephesians 5:26 – Jesus cleansed the church by the **washing of water** with the **word**. (1 Corinthians 12:13)

So "born of water and the Spirit" means one is born again when he is baptized in water in obedience to the gospel message revealed by the Holy Spirit! That is simple, clear, and agrees with passage after passage found elsewhere.

Conclusions

Baptism Must Be Done for the Proper Purpose.

Baptism is not just an outer act. It has a vital spiritual meaning, as we have learned. God wants obedience from proper motives (Romans 6:17,18; 1 Corinthians 4:15; John 4:24).

Compare this to the Lord's Supper. In the communion we outwardly eat the bread and drink the cup, but we must inwardly recognize it to be a memorial to Jesus' body and blood. If we fail to recognize this inner spiritual meaning, we are condemned even though we physically eat and drink (1 Corinthian 11:26-29). Likewise, to receive the intended benefit of baptism, we must do it for the proper purpose.

Suppose a person is baptized believing the common doctrine that he is born again **before** or without baptism. Would he be baptized for the proper reasons: "for the remission of sins" (Acts 2:38), so the blood of Jesus could cleanse his sins (Acts 22:16), and so he could become a child of God (Romans 6:3,4; Galatians 3:26,27; etc.)? No. His baptism would be unscriptural because it was done for the wrong reasons, even if his outward action was right.

But we have learned that baptism is necessary to be born again, so what is the condition of one whose baptism was not valid? Is he born again? Is he a child of God? How could he be, when he has not obeyed the only true seed that can make him a child of God (1 Peter 1:22,23; Luke 8:11)? He needs to do what was done by the twelve men in Acts

19:1-5. They had been "baptized" (immersed) but without proper understanding of its purpose. So they needed to be baptized Scripturally.

Churches Must Teach Truth about the New Birth.

Many churches teach that we are born again before baptism or without baptism. What about people who obey the doctrine taught by such groups? They have not done what Jesus said to do to be born again! Then what is their condition?

Remember that one is born again only if he obeys the proper seed, the true gospel. Should a person continue to be part of a group that misleads people about such a basic question as how to become a child of God? Consider again 2 John 9-11; Galatians 1:8,9; Matthew 15:9,14; etc.

A Child of God Must Faithfully Serve His Father.

Romans 6:4 – One who has been born again must "walk in newness of life." Being "born again" is not the final goal; it must be just the beginning of a lifetime of obedient service. It is not enough just to be forgiven. One must live a life of faithful obedience.

A child of God must submit to His Father (1 Peter 2:1,2; Matthew 12:50; 2 Corinthians 6:17,18; 1 John 3:1-10). He must be active in His Father's family, the church (1 Timothy 3:15). As a child of God, he must grow up in Christ (2 Peter 3:18).

Have you been truly born again? If so, are you serving the Father faithfully? Do you need to make corrections?

Will All Devout, Moral People Be Saved?

Introduction:

When the practices or teachings of a religious group are shown to violate Scripture, often someone will respond that the people involved are zealous religious people and/or good moral people. The intended message is that these folks are acceptable to God simply because they have good morals and religious zeal, despite their continued disobedience to God's word. The conclusion is that people should not criticize the beliefs or practices of such otherwise good people.

The Bible absolutely does teach that people should be religiously devout and should have good morals, but are those things enough to assure that they will receive eternal life? To illustrate, every citizen of the United States is a living human, but just because someone is a living human, does that prove he is a US citizen? Likewise, a person must have religious zeal and good morals to please God, but is this enough for him to be saved or is something more required in addition to this?

Consider several areas of Bible teaching that relate to this subject.

Consider Some Bible Examples.

Does the Bible say that God was always pleased with people who were dedicated to their religion and lived good moral lives? Or were some people unsaved despite having good morals and religious devotion? Consider several Bible examples.

The Ethiopian Treasurer - Acts 8:26-39

This man was dedicated to his religion even before he heard the gospel.

He had traveled by chariot from Ethiopia to Jerusalem in order to worship (verse 27). As he traveled, he read the Scriptures (verse 28) and wanted to understand them better (verses 30-34).

But was he saved and destined for eternal life at this time?

He did not even know about Jesus.

Philip had to teach him about Jesus (verse 35). Can one be saved while he does not believe in Jesus?

Acts 4:12 – There is salvation in no other name but that of Jesus.

John 8:24 – Those who do not believe in Jesus will die in sin. How then could the treasurer have been saved before he believed? (Compare John 14:6; Mark 16:16.)

Further, he had not yet been baptized.

Philip had to baptize him (verses 36-39). Can a person be in a saved state before he has been baptized?

Mark 16:16 – We must believe and be baptized in order to be saved.

Acts 2:38 – We must repent and be baptized in order to have the remission of sins.

The eunuch was dedicated to his religion, yet he was unsaved until he heard the gospel of Jesus, believed it, and was baptized.

(See also Acts 22:16; Romans 6:3,4; Galatians 3:27; 1 Peter 3:21.)

Saul of Tarsus - Acts 22:3-16

Saul was also zealous in his religion even before he became a Christian.

He was a strict Jew, zealous toward God (22:3). He lived in all good conscience (23:1). He had been a "Hebrew of Hebrews," blameless according to the law (Philippians 3:5,6). He advanced in the Jews' religion beyond his peers, because he was more zealous for the traditions of the fathers (Galatians 1:13,14). Surely he was religiously devout.

But was Saul saved in this condition?

He did not believe Jesus was the Christ, the Savior.

In fact, he persecuted Jesus' disciples (Acts 8:1-3; 9:1,2; 22:4,5), and did many things contrary to Jesus' name (Acts 26:9). He was a blasphemer, a persecutor, and injurious (1 Timothy 1:13). At this point, he was the "chief of sinners" (1 Timothy 1:15).

Even after he believed, he was in sin till he was baptized.

Acts 22:16 – He was commanded: "arise and be baptized and wash away your sins."

Like the Ethiopian, Saul was also a zealous religious person, yet he was unsaved until he believed in Jesus and obeyed Him by being baptized.

Cornelius - Acts 10 and 11

Cornelius was a religious, moral man before he heard the gospel.

He was devout, feared God, gave alms, and prayed to God (10:2). He was righteous, feared God, and was respected by the Jews (10:22). If just being religious and having high morals would save a man, Cornelius would have been saved long before Peter preached the gospel to him.

But was Cornelius saved before he heard and obeyed the gospel?

God told him to send for Peter who would tell him words whereby he might be saved (11:14). Peter came, taught him about Jesus, and commanded him to be baptized in water (10:47,48).

So Cornelius was yet another good moral man, religiously active and dedicated, who was unsaved till he heard gospel, believed in Jesus, and was baptized.

The Athenians - Acts 17:16-31

These people too were zealous religious people.

Their city was filled with idols that the people worshiped religiously (17:16). They were so zealous they even put up an altar to "the unknown god" in case they missed one (17:23).

But were these idol worshipers saved in that condition?

17:29-31 – Paul taught that their idolatry was wrong, and people must repent of it to be acceptable in the judgment. Was Paul wrong to show them they were religiously in error?

1 Corinthians 6:9-11; Galatians 5:19-21 – Idolaters will not inherit the kingdom of God.

Revelation 21:8; 22:15 – Instead, idolaters will be in the lake of fire, the second death.

Idol worshipers are religious, often very devout, and some have good morals. If that is all people need, why are idolaters not saved?

The Jews - Romans 10:1-3

These Jews were zealous in their religion.

They had a zeal for God (10:2). They had a system of religion, although it was human in origin (10:3). Even today, many Jews are very devoted to their religion, and many are good moral people.

But was their religious zeal enough to save them?

They did not know God's way for making men righteous (the gospel of Jesus), so they did not submit to God's righteousness (10:3). Therefore, they needed to be saved (10:1). Jews, of course, do not believe in Jesus, so they do not obey Him. We have already studied verses showing that obedient faith is necessary to salvation.

Surely it should be clear that people are not necessarily saved just because they are devoted to some religious system or just because they have good morals. Other things are necessary, including knowledge of the gospel, faith in Jesus, and obedience to the gospel of Jesus Christ (Romans 1:16).

Consider the Bible Teaching about Truth and Error.

If a person is saved simply because he actively practices some religious faith and lives a good moral life, regardless of the content of his faith, then it would not matter whether or not he practiced religious truth. He could be saved just by being religious, regardless of whether or not that religion harmonized with the Bible. But consider the Bible teaching.

The Importance of Religious Truth

Proverbs 23:23 – Buy the **truth** and sell it not. Truth is worth any sacrifice you must make to obtain it. Once you have truth, you must not give it up no matter what you could gain by giving it up. But if being religiously zealous is all that matters, why be so concerned about truth?

John 8:31,32 – To be free from sin, we must know and abide in **truth**. Note that Jesus said this even to people who believed in Him. But what if we think that truth is not important as long as we have religious zeal? Will we still be made free from sin?

1 Peter 1:22,23 – To be made free from sin and be born again, we must obey the **truth**, which is God's word. What if we are religiously zealous, but have obeyed error instead of the truth? Would our religious zeal alone save us? No, we must obey the truth to be saved.

2 John 9-11 – To have fellowship with the Father and Son, we must abide in Jesus' teaching. What if we are religious, but our religion is not in harmony with Jesus' teaching? Then we do not have God!

If you are religious, that is good. But do you also have the truth? (John 4:23,24)

The Danger of Religious Error

Matthew 7:15,21-23 – Many people have been deceived by false teachers. As a result they call Jesus "Lord," teach in His name, and do many wonderful works in His name. Yet they are lost. How could this be if the only thing needed is religious zeal? Clearly something more is needed. What is it? We must "do the will of the Father."

2 Corinthians 11:13-15 – Satan and his servants pretend to be ministers of light and apostles of Christ. If such men deceive us, we will be religious but will be following Satan! Does Satan lead people to eternal life? It is possible to be religious and yet be following Satan, because Satan is a deceiver. He fools people into following counterfeit religious practices, thinking they will still be saved.

Galatians 1:6-9 – People who teach a different gospel are accursed, and those who accept that gospel are departing from Him who called them. These Galatians were religious. In fact, they even believed in Jesus and were children of God (3:26,27). They followed a "gospel," but were accursed because it was a different gospel. Someone was teaching them they must still obey Old Testament circumcision; this would cause them to fall from grace (5:1-4).

1 Timothy 4:1-3 – Some people fall away, following doctrines of demons, speaking lies, including some specific false doctrines listed. Yet these people are religious. They follow religious commandments, yet they fall away because they follow commands that are not from God.

1 John 4:1 – Many false prophets are in the world, so we should not believe all teachers but put them to the test. Why should we put teachers to the test? In fact, why should we even care whether we are following false teaching or true teaching, if the only thing that matters is that we be religious?

Matthew 15:9 – People may even worship the one true God, yet their worship would be vain if it was based on humanly originated practices. (Note also verse 14.)

Suppose a person is very dedicated in taking medicine to cure a disease. Would he be cured simply because he was dedicated, even if it is the wrong medicine? So religious zeal is necessary, but by itself it is not enough. It is possible even for believers in Jesus Christ to be deceived into following error and false teaching.

Consider the Bible Teaching about Unity and Division.

There are religiously zealous and good moral people in all kinds of different religious faiths. If religious zeal and good morals were all we need, then people who cause, promote, and justify division would still be saved.

In fact, this is the main reason why people claim that all devout, good moral people will be saved: they want to believe that people can be saved in any denomination, despite the fact that denominations are divided in practice, worship, organization, plan of salvation, etc. When we rebuke these divisions (and the false doctrines that produce them), that's when people say we should hush, because these are devout, good moral people. In other words, one of the main reasons people promote the idea is to justify people who are religiously divided!

What does the Bible say?

The Importance of Unity

John 17:20-23 – Jesus prayed for all to be one as He and the Father are one. If religious zeal and good morals are all we need to be saved, why did He pray for religious unity? Why didn't He just pray for everyone to be zealously devout and have good morals? When people say that doctrinal differences do not matter, they are contradicting Jesus' prayer and justifying the very division that He sought to eliminate.

Ephesians 4:3-6 – We must strive for unity according to the Spirit, in the bond of peace. This requires oneness in each of the seven areas listed, including one God, one faith, and one body (which is the church – 1:22,23). If religious zeal and good morals were all we need to be saved, why strive for unity? But the Bible says that unity matters.

We need religious zeal, but we also need religious unity. That unity requires all believers to follow one faith and be members of one church, just as surely as we must believe in one God.

The Danger of Division

1 Corinthians 1:10-13 – Since Jesus is not divided against Himself, it follows that His followers should not be divided. There should be no divisions among us such as those that existed at Corinth. But the division that exists today between denominations is far greater than what existed at Corinth, and yet some people say we should just overlook what the Scriptures expressly forbid!

If religious zeal is all we need, why does this passage rebuke division? If Paul believed like some people today, he would have told the Corinthians their divisions did not matter as long as they were zealous!

Galatians 5:19-21 – We need to be good moral people, because those who do not practice moral purity will not inherit the kingdom of God. But the same passage says that those who cause division will likewise not inherit the kingdom of God!

Yes, good morals are essential. But people today are mistaken when they say religious division does not matter as long as people are morally good and religiously zealous. God's word says that practicing and excusing division is as bad as being immoral. And yet the primary reason the doctrine we are studying even exists is so people have a way to justify those who are religiously divided!

Conclusion

Perhaps you are a good moral person, zealous for your religious practices. If so, these are good qualities. God approves of zeal and good morals. But please understand that, by themselves, these qualities will only leave you where they left Saul, Cornelius, and the Ethiopian before they learned and obeyed the truth. Even if you believe that Jesus Christ is God's Son and man's Savior, that is still not enough unless you believe and obey the rest of the gospel teaching about salvation and the church.

You need to be sure you have the truth, obey the true gospel, and unite with other faithful Christians in Jesus' one true church. Otherwise, you are like a man in Chicago who wants to travel to New York, so with zeal and dedication he drives down the highway that leads to Los Angeles. No matter how zealous and dedicated he may be, the truth is that he is going in the wrong direction. In order to reach his destination, he must turn around and go the right direction.

Have you obeyed the true teachings of Jesus' gospel in order to receive forgiveness of your sins? Are you following His true plan for faithful service to Him in His true church?

A New Man

The Gospel of Change

Introduction:

I once read the following statement (paraphrased): "Jesus never left anyone the same. Of everyone who ever met Him, He demanded change" (*Christian Counselors Manual*, page 247). Think of all the people whom Jesus demanded to change: the apostles, Nicodemus, the rich young ruler, the Samaritan woman, the woman taken in adultery, the scribes and Pharisees, Saul of Tarsus. Some heeded His call for change and some did not, but He required them all to change.

Change is a fundamental concept of the gospel of Christ.

The gospel repeatedly emphasizes that those who are in Christ must be new and different.

2 Corinthians 5:17 – If anyone is in Christ, he is a **new** creation; old things have passed away; behold, all things have become **new**.

Romans 6:4 – We were buried with Him through baptism into death, that just as Christ was raised from the dead by the glory of the Father, even so we also should walk in **newness** of life.

The purpose of this lesson is to consider the gospel teaching that requires us to be new and different people.

Many people tend to resist change. Even people who know that the Bible teaches the importance of a new life as Christians, may resist specific changes in our lives. And when we try to make changes, we find change difficult.

Consider the following aspects of the Bible teaching about the need for change:

The Importance of Change

Consider some of the gospel concepts that emphasize the need for change.

A new man and a new birth

2 Corinthians 5:17 – When one comes into Christ, he becomes a **new creature**. Old things are passed away and all things become **new**. We must not continue in the old ways. Those have passed away. We must look at everything about our lives in a new way so we change as needed.

John 3:3,5 – This change is the result of a **new birth**. Becoming a follower of Christ is like being born again. It is like starting life all over again. Jesus intends for each of us to become an entirely new and different person.

Romans 6:4 – When we are buried with Christ in baptism, we walk in **newness** of life.

Baptism is not just about being forgiven of sins. It is the final step of a process in which we commit ourselves to change, and it is the beginning of a whole new life which must lead us to be different from what we were and different from the people of the world.

Transformation

Romans 12:2 – Do not be conformed to this world, but be **transformed** by the renewing of your mind. Transformation involves a complete change of nature, like a caterpillar being changed into a butterfly. That is how you and I must change to please God.

2 Corinthians 3:18 – Beholding as in a mirror the glory of the Lord, we are being **transformed** into the same image from glory to glory, just as by the Spirit of the Lord. As we observe our Master, our goal is to become like Him. That requires major change.

People in society often talk about the need for change: change in healthcare, change in the economy, change in politics, etc. But not all change is good. The goal is not change for the sake of change. Nevertheless, change is absolutely essential to the gospel.

Becoming a Christian is not just about changing from guilty to innocent. It is about being transformed into different people, so that we become like our Master. And baptism is not the conclusion of this change. Baptism is the beginning of a lifetime of change.

Repentance and works of repentance

Repentance is a fundamental step in changing, because repentance is a change of mind. Repentance is when we **determine** to become different. To change, we must be transformed by renewing our mind. We determine in our hearts that we will change.

Acts 2:38 – **Repent** and be baptized in the name of Jesus Christ for the remission of sins.

2 Corinthians 7:10 – Godly sorrow produces **repentance** leading to salvation.

Acts 8:22 – **Repent** therefore of this your wickedness, and pray God if perhaps the thought of your heart may be forgiven you.

Acts 26:20 – Men must then do **works** worthy of **repentance**. (Luke 3:8-14; Matthew 3:8)

Repentance is not just a requirement before baptism. Most of these passages are addressed to followers of Christ. Repentance is needed repeatedly in our lives whenever we sin. It is a fundamental part of the ongoing process of change in the Christian's life.

Conversion

We often refer to the process of becoming a follower of Christ as "conversion." But the basic meaning of the term refers to a fundamental change.

Psalms 19:7 – The law of the Lord is perfect, **converting** the soul.

Matthew 18:3 – Unless you are **converted** and become as little children, you will by no means enter the kingdom of heaven.

Acts 3:19 – Repent therefore and be **converted**, that your sins may be blotted out.

The reason we needed to be converted is that each of us was guilty of sin, which alienated us from God. So we must change our relationship with God, but to do so we must change our course.

The life of a Christian begins with a change from sin to righteousness, from guilt to innocence, from separation from God to reconciliation to God, from being lost to being saved. But this is just the beginning of a lifetime of change. To resist or neglect to change where we need to change is to reject the fundamental concept which made us Christians to begin with.

Growth

After becoming a child of God, we must grow as Christians. But growth is change.

John 15:2 – Every branch that bears fruit He prunes, that it may bear **more fruit**.

Ephesians 4:15 – Speaking the truth in love, may **grow up** in all things into Him who is the head, Christ.

2 Peter 3:18 – **Grow** in the grace and knowledge of our Lord and Savior Jesus Christ.

After conversion, a Christian must live a life of growth. We must totally re-examine every aspect of our lives: moral conduct, church membership, Bible study, prayer and all aspects of worship, conduct toward our spouse and children, employer and other employees, neighbors and civil rulers. We must change our action, speech, dress, and especially attitude. Anything that does not harmonize with the word of God must change.

One who is unwilling to change or who neglects to change, can never become what God wants him to be. Change is absolutely fundamental to the gospel of Christ and to the life of a Christian.

I want to emphasize two fundamental principles we need to make the necessary changes.

Putting Off the Old and Putting on the New

Ephesians 4:22-24 – Put off, concerning your former conduct, the old man which grows corrupt according to the deceitful lusts, and be renewed in the spirit of your mind, and put on the new man which was created according to God, in true righteousness and holiness. (Colossians 3:9,10)

The change that the gospel requires involves both putting off and putting on. Some passages tell us things we must cease or eliminate from our lives. Other passages tell us things we must add and improve in our lives. And some passages tell us to both put off and put on.

Note Examples:

Passage	Put Off	Put On
Ephesians 4:25	Putting away lying	speak truth with his neighbor
Ephesians 4:28	Let him who stole, Steal no longer	but labor, to give him who has need
Ephesians 4:29	Let no corrupt word proceed out of your mouth	but what is good for edification, that it may impart grace to the hearers.
Ephesians 4:31,32	Let all bitterness, wrath, anger, clamor, and evil speaking be put away, with all malice.	And be kind to one another, tenderhearted, forgiving one another, just as God in Christ forgave you
Psalm 1:1,2	Blessed is the man who walks not in the counsel of the ungodly,	but his delight is in the law of the LORD, and in His law he meditates
Proverbs 15:28	But the mouth of the wicked pours forth evil	The heart of the righteous studies how to

		answer
James 1:21	Lay aside all filthiness and overflow of wickedness	receive with meekness the implanted word, which is able to save your souls.
James 5:12	Do not swear	but let your "Yes," be "Yes," and your "No," "No."
Hebrews 10:25	Not forsaking the assembling of ourselves together	but exhorting one another
1 Peter 2:1,2	Laying aside all malice, all deceit, hypocrisy, envy, and evil speaking	desire the pure milk of the word, that you may grow thereby
1 Peter 3:9	Not returning evil for evil or reviling for reviling	but on the contrary blessing
Romans 6:12,13	do not present your members as instruments of unrighteousness to sin	but present yourselves to God, and your members as instruments of righteousness to God
Galatians 5:19-24	Those who do the works of the flesh will not inherit the kingdom	But the fruit of the Spirit is ...

Lessons to Be Learned

Gospel change requires both eliminating evil and adding positive good works.

Many people seem to think that doing some good will compensate for their sins.

Immoral people may feel justified because they donate to charitable works, help their neighbors, or work hard on their jobs. For example, some people tell how kind and generous their homosexual friends are, as though somehow good works compensate for homosexuality.

When you point out the errors of a religious group, members may tell about the good works the group is doing, as though that means their sins should not be criticized.

On the other hand, people in faithful congregations may neglect positive works of service, but they think they should be accepted because they are not involved in moral or religious error.

As we have seen, the gospel requires a complete new man. This requires both eliminating evil and diligently practicing good works.

Both are necessary, and neglecting either one is a failure to change as God's word teaches.

Adding good supports and encourages removing evil, and vice-versa.

Matthew 12:43-45 – A demon left a man but later found the man's life still empty. He moved back in bringing seven other demons with him! Jesus applied this to Israel, but it is a general principle. Replace bad habits with good and the bad is less likely to return.

Removing evil and adding good tend to encourage and strengthen one another. A person who attempts to do good will find that any evil that remains in his life will hinder his good works.

On the other hand, as with the man with the demons, our attempts to remove evil will be more successful if we replace the sin with good works. For every bad habit you "put off," find some useful activity to "put on" in its place, and keeping out the evil will be much easier.

Proper change involves both removing evil and adding good. Put off and put on.

Practice Makes Perfect

Success in changing ourselves to please God requires just plain hard work and diligent practice. This is especially so if sin has become habitual in our lives or if we need some good work to become a habit. God does not promise change will be easy, but He promises it is possible if we work diligently according to His word.

So in order to change to serve God, we must compel ourselves to do what we know is right and repeat it until it becomes "second nature."

Consider Some Scriptures.

Diligence and hard work

1 Corinthians 15:58 — Be steadfast, immovable, always abounding in the **work** of the Lord.

James 1:22-25 — Be **doers** of the word, not just hearers.

Luke 9:23 – If anyone desires to come after Me, let him deny himself, and take up his cross **daily**, and follow Me.

Exercise and training

The changes we need to make are often described like the training programs and practice that athletes must use to develop their skill.

Hebrews 5:14 – But solid food belongs to those who are of full age, that is, those who by reason of **use** have their senses **exercised** to discern both good and evil.

Luke 6:40 – A disciple is not above his teacher, but everyone who is perfectly ***trained*** will be like his teacher.

1 Timothy 4:7,8 – ***Exercise*** yourself toward godliness. For bodily exercise profits a little, but godliness is profitable for all things, having promise of the life that now is and of that which is to come. (NASB: "discipline yourself")

1 Corinthians 9:27 – But I ***discipline*** my body and bring it into subjection, lest, when I have preached to others, I myself should become disqualified.

Most of us have some understanding of the exercise and practice that athletes undergo in order to be winners. In comparison to a sport, becoming a godly person is far more important. But in a similar way it requires persistent hard work.

(2 Timothy 3:16,17)

Lessons to Be Learned

Habits are formed by repeated action.

Changing to become a righteous person will require repeated, diligent practice and training in doing right instead of wrong. This is true in the formation of any habit. Our bad habits developed by repetition of bad practices. In the same way, in order to break our bad habits and establish good habits, we must diligently practice good instead of bad.

At first this requires conscious, deliberate effort and may not feel comfortable or natural. We may need to force ourselves to do right instead of wrong until it becomes second nature.

Consider how you learned to ride a bicycle or drive a car. At first you had to consciously control each action, even when it felt unnatural and uncomfortable. You had to think about each step, and make yourself do what needed to be done. But repetition produces habits that soon feel natural.

The same is true in spiritual matters. When we first cease our sinful practices and begin doing good works, we may feel strange. Our old ways may seem comfortable because we are used to them. New ways may seem uncomfortable and unnatural. This may be true of attending church meetings, studying the Bible, prayer, teaching others, and leading in the worship assemblies of the church. Each new step may seem strange.

But as we learn them by continual use and practice, we find that it soon becomes a part of our lives. Then we would not feel right if we went back to our old way of life.

Success in change requires persistence and patience.

The kind of serious and significant change that the gospel requires often takes time. That is why the Scriptures describe it as a growth process.

Growth does not happen overnight. It often involves mistakes, stumbling, and even falling. Consider how our children learn to walk and run and eventually become useful workers. So, we must not let our problems and failures keep us from getting up and going on.

Likewise, the athlete does not learn his skill in just a few attempts. His training requires discipline and diligence. He must practice his skills day in and day out to achieve his goals.

The Christian has far greater goals to accomplish. His change requires becoming a fundamentally new person in his conduct, his speech, his dress, and his whole outlook on life.

And every change requires action: we must **act** to eliminate sinful practices, **act** to develop good habits, **act** to improve our attitudes, **act** to improve our speech, **act** to learn to help those around us. Christ requires change, and change requires action. And we must persist in the action till we succeed.

Conclusion

Acts 17:30 says God commands all men everywhere to repent. But repentance is a decision to change. So God requires all people everywhere to make up their mind to change and turn from sin. This is not just a surface change or tweaking a few habits here and there. It is a fundamental change of one's entire character and outlook on life from the inside out.

People who have never become Christians must repent of their past sins and make up their minds to receive forgiveness by the blood of Jesus Christ. This requires them to confess Christ and be baptized for the forgiveness of sins. Then they must bring forth the fruits of repentance by diligently changing their lives to become faithful followers of Christ.

But those who are already Christians must continue this lifetime of change and growth. And they also must repent when they find that they have failed to change as they ought to. Then they must pray for forgiveness and make correction with those against whom they have sinned.

Please consider your own life and determine to make the changes that God requires.

The Importance of Jesus' Church

Our society increasingly sees the church as irrelevant or unnecessary.

* Many say, "I'm a good moral person. I believe in God and treat my family and neighbors right. Why do I need to be a member of the church?"

* People see denominational division or hypocrisy, so they reject the whole idea of the church.

* Many young people reject "organized religion." Those who claim to be religious and even believe in Jesus may want nothing to do with the church.

Members of denominations often contribute to this thinking.

* Some say, "The church cannot save you. Christ saves you. We need Christianity, not churchianity." But what they mean is that church membership is not essential to salvation.

* In order to justify their divisions, denominations may say, "It doesn't matter **which** church you attend, as long as you worship God." So, people conclude they don't need to be a member of **any** church at all.

* Premillennialism says Jesus came to set up His kingdom but failed because people rejected Him. So He changed His plan and set up the church. This makes the church an unplanned substitute, which God never really intended. That does not make it very important.

* Some church members think we should teach unsaved people about forgiveness, but should not teach about the church till after they are saved.

The purpose of this study is to consider the importance of the church you can read about in your New Testament.

We do not claim that denominations are needed. Denominations are not found in the New Testament and were never part of God's plan. They were added by men hundreds of years after Jesus' church began. We can and should be saved without joining any denomination.

Nor are we saying that the ***people*** in the church make the church important. We will see that the church is important because of its relationship to ***God*** and its role in the plan of ***God***.

But the gospel describes the church that Jesus planned and built and to which He added people in the New Testament. What about that church? How important is it to our salvation?

Consider:

Terms Used to Describe the Church

Various terms are used for the church.

The House (Family) of God

The church is called the house(hold) of God.

Ephesians 2:16,19 – Jesus reconciled Jew and Gentile to God in one body through the cross. Therefore, we are fellow citizens with the saints and members of the ***household*** of God.

1 Timothy 3:15 – Paul wrote so we may know how to conduct ourselves in the ***house*** of God, which is the church of the living God.

(2 Corinthians 6:18; 1 John 3:1,2; Galatians 6:10)

Why is it important to be in the house of God?

People become members of God's family by being "born again."

1 Peter 1:22,23 – When we obey God's word, we purify our souls and are born again. But this new birth makes us children of God, and children of God are members of His family, the church. What does that mean about those who are not members of the church?

Galatians 3:26,27 – We ***are*** children of God by faith, because we ***were*** baptized into Christ. Baptism makes us children of God, members of God's family (1 Corinthians 12:13).

Many people teach that people need to be "born again," but they often think church membership does not matter. These folks need to consider the fact that being born again makes us members of the family of God and that family is the church.

Only children of God will receive God's eternal inheritance.

1 Peter 1:3,4 – God has **begotten** us to an inheritance reserved for us in heaven.

Romans 8:16,17 – Children of God are heirs of God and joint heirs with Christ.

The church does not give the inheritance. **God** gives the inheritance. But **to whom** does He give it? To His children, members of His family. But His family is the church.

If it is important to be born again, to be children of God, and to receive the inheritance from God, then church membership is important, because the church is the family of God.

The Body of Christ

The church is the body of Christ.

Ephesians 1:22,23 – Christ is head of the church, which is His body.

(Colossians 1:18,24)

Why do we need to be members of Christ's body?

Christ is Head of the body (Ephesians 1:22,23; Colossians 1:18)

Christ is the Head of only **one** institution. There is **one body** (Ephesians 4:4-6), just as there is only one God and Father. Is Christ the Head of an unimportant, non-essential institution? To belittle the body is to belittle its Head!

Christ is Savior of the body.

Ephesians 5:23 – Christ is head of the church, being the **Savior of the body**.

Ephesians 5:25 – He loved the church and **gave Himself for it**.

The church is the body of Christ, and Christ is the Savior of the body. What does that mean about people who are not in the body (church)?

It is true that the **church** does not save us. **Christ** saves us. But **whom** does He save? The **church**! The church is the body of all people who have been saved by the blood of Jesus.

(Acts 2:47; Ephesians 2:16; Colossians 3:15)

The Kingdom of Christ

To be in Jesus' church is to be a citizen in His kingdom.

Matthew 16:18,19 – Jesus promised to build His **church** and give Peter the keys of the **kingdom**. The terms are used interchangeably.

Colossians 1:13 – God translated those who are saved into the kingdom of His dear Son.

(Revelation 1:8; Hebrews 12:23,28)

Why do we need to be citizens in Jesus' kingdom?

The kingdom is a fundamental part of the gospel.

Matthew 3:2; 4:23 – Both John and Jesus emphasized preaching the gospel of the kingdom.

Acts 8:12; 19:8 – Philip and Paul also preached about the kingdom when they preached the gospel. People who say we should not preach about the church to non-Christians need to consider these passages. (20:25; 28:23,31)

The truth is that we cannot preach the true gospel of Christ without preaching about the kingdom (church). To attempt to preach the gospel without preaching the church would be to preach a different gospel (Galatians 1:8).

The kingdom consists of those who have been delivered from the power of darkness – Colossians 1:12-14.

Darkness is a symbol of sin. In the kingdom we are qualified to partake of the inheritance of the saints, because Christ redeemed and forgave us.

Many religious people look forward eagerly to the kingdom, but fail to appreciate the church. They need to realize that the kingdom now exists. It is the church. And all who have been saved from the power of darkness are citizens in that kingdom, the church.

(See also Matthew 6:33; 13:44,45.)

The terms used to describe the church demonstrate that all saved people are in the church. The church is absolutely essential to salvation.

The Plans Laid for the Church

The church is part of the eternal purpose of God.

The Church Was Purposed by God from Eternity.

Ephesians 3:10,11 – The church is a major part of God's eternal purpose, demonstrating God's wisdom. Those who view the church as a last-minute substitute are mistaken.

A beautiful painting reveals the skill of the artist. A powerful rocket reveals the wisdom of its makers. So the church reveals the wisdom of God as part of His eternal purpose. To say the church is not essential is to say that the eternal purpose of God is not essential.

The Church Was Prophesied in the Old Testament.

Isaiah 2:2,3 – The Lord's house would be established in the last days, when the law went forth from Jerusalem. Remember that God's house is the church.

Daniel 2:31-45 – Nebuchadnezzar dreamed of an image. It prophesied that the kingdom (church) would begin during the Roman Empire.

God planned the church centuries before it began. Would the Creator and Ruler of the Universe go to such trouble for an insignificant institution?

(Zechariah 6:12,13; 1 Corinthians 3:16; 2 Corinthians 6:16; etc.)

Jesus Promised to Build the Church.

Matthew 16:18 – Jesus promised to build His church.
(Compare 4:23 and references to the kingdom.)

People put great effort into planning something only if it is important to them.

A bride makes many plans because she considers her wedding ceremony to be important.

Auto makers spend much time and effort in planning new models.

So Jesus put much effort into planning the church. Clearly it was important to Him.

In particular, He came to save men from sin – Luke 19:10. (5:32; Matthew 20:28)

But while here He carefully prepared people for the church/kingdom.

God planned to save men from sin, and Jesus came to work that plan. The church is an essential part of that plan. It follows that the church is essential to our salvation.

The Price Paid for the Church

The Church Was Purchased by Jesus' Blood.

Acts 20:28 – He purchased the church with His blood.

Ephesians 5:23,25 – He is Savior of the body (church), because He gave Himself for it.

Matthew 16:18 – For this reason it is **His** church, belonging to Him.

(Romans 16:16; Colossians 1:13; 1 Corinthians 6:19,20)

How Important Is Jesus' Death?

The price someone is willing to pay for something shows its value to him.

    * Where food is scarce, people work most of their time to provide it.

    * People pay exorbitant fees for operations that may save their lives.

    * But we would pay little for something we do not value. Some people pay a fortune for "modern art," but I wouldn't pay a dime!

The highest price anyone can pay for anything is his life.

When a soldier or policeman dies in the line of duty, he has paid "the supreme price."

If a father dies trying to rescue his family, he paid the highest price he could pay.

So Jesus bought the church by paying the highest price anyone could pay.

The importance of a death is determined by the importance of the person.

All souls are of equal value to God, but some deaths have more serious consequences.

    * To an army, the death of a general is more important than that of a private.

    * To a nation, the death of a king would be a greater loss than the death of a beggar.

Consider then the death of Jesus. He was not just the greatest man that ever lived, He was more than a man. He was God in the flesh, the only-begotten Son of God. If He died to purchase the church, consider how valuable and important He must consider the church!

Consider the purpose of Jesus' death.

    Jesus died to save us from our sins.

Ephesians 1:7 – We have redemption through His blood, even the forgiveness of sins.

Matthew 26:28 – He shed His blood for many for remission of sins. (1 Peter 2:24)

    Jesus died to save us, but He purchased the church with His blood.

Surely this makes the church essential to salvation. This is why Ephesians 5 says He is Savior of the body.

Acts 2:47 – The Lord adds the saved to the church. When one is forgiven of sins by Jesus' blood, Jesus puts him in the church. So, the church is the body of people who have been saved and purchased by Jesus' death.

People who say the church is not essential to salvation are unintentionally saying that Jesus' death is not essential. How dare anyone say that the church is not important, when Jesus died to purchase the church!

The Work Done by the Church

The main work of the church is spiritual, to help people have a right relationship with God.

Worship

The church conducts assemblies in which people gather to worship God.

We partake of the Lord's Supper in church assemblies.

1 Corinthians 10:16,17 – Those who partake of the bread are members of Christ's body. (Luke 22:29,30; 1 Corinthians 11:18-22)

We also sing and pray in the church assemblies.

1 Corinthians 14:15 – Paul taught us to sing and pray in church assemblies.

This can be done outside the assemblies, but should also be done when the church meets.
(verse 19; Hebrews 2:12)

How important is this worship?

John 4:23,24 – God seeks people to worship Him in spirit and in truth.

Hebrews 10:25 – We should not forsake our assembling together. (1 Corinthians 11:23-26)

To receive our Father's inheritance, we must serve Him faithfully. This requires fulfilling **group** responsibilities. It is not enough just to live good lives and worship God at home. We cannot receive eternal life without fulfilling our God-given work in the church.

Preaching the Gospel

The church is God's ordained institution for preaching the gospel.

1 Timothy 3:15 – The church is the pillar and ground of the truth.

2 Corinthians 11:8; Philippians 4:15,16 – Churches sent funds to support preachers.
(Acts 11:26; Hebrews 10:24,25; 1 Corinthians 14)

How important is the preaching of the gospel?

Romans 10:17 – Faith comes by hearing the gospel.

Mark 16:15,16 – Men must hear to believe and be baptized.

Matthew 28:20 – Men must be taught to observe all Jesus' commands.

(Romans 1:16; John 6:44,45; 8:32)

The most important thing you can do for another person is to help him save his soul. And the only way to do that is to teach him the gospel (by word and example). This is the primary work of the church. It is the most important work any institution can do.

Conclusion

Again, the point is not that membership in some denomination is essential.

On the contrary, denominations are no part of God's plan. The church that is essential is the body of all saved people which God planned and Jesus built. It is the kingdom of Christ, the family of God.

The church is important because God chose to make it important.

* If it is important to be saved from sin and become children of God, then the church is important, because only those who are in the church have these blessings.

* If the purpose of God is important, then the church is important, because the church is a fundamental part of God's eternal purpose.

* If Jesus' death is important, then the church is important, because Jesus died for the church.

* If worship and gospel preaching are important, then the church is important, because these are what the Lord established the church to accomplish.

The church is important because of its relationship to God and to Jesus.

* The church is the family of **God,** the body and kingdom of **Christ**.

* The church fulfills the purpose of **God**.

* The church was purchased by the blood of **Jesus**.

* The church exists to worship **God** and preach **His** message.

Again, the church is not important because of the *people* in the church. It is important because the Father and Son are important and the church sustains an essential relationship to Them. To exalt the church is not to belittle God but to exalt God and respect His will.

The value we see in the church is reflected in our participation in church activities. Have you been added to Jesus' church by receiving forgiveness of your sins by the blood of Christ? How diligent are you in participating in church worship assemblies and study opportunities?

Let Us Return to the Lord

Introduction:

God's people in the Old Testament often left God's ways to go into error. When this happened, God did not immediately abandon them as impossible to reclaim. He urged them to repent and return, so He could forgive them.

Isaiah 55:6,7 – The wicked should forsake their ways and return to the Lord. He will have mercy and will abundantly pardon.

Hosea 6:1 – "Come and let us return unto the Lord."

Likewise today some people begin serving God but then go into error, and God still calls such people to repent so He can forgive them.

The purpose of this study is to consider the need for some children of God to be restored. In nearly every community and in nearly every local church there are erring children of God who need to repent of sin. Often these people know they are guilty. The Lord cares about such people and so should the Lord's people. We urge all members to consider whether they need to return to the Lord.

Christians Must Remain Faithful to Receive Eternal Life.

Becoming a child of God is just the beginning. To enter heaven, we must continue to live a lifetime of service to God.

Serving God Must Be Priority.

Romans 12:1,2 – Do not conform to the world, but present your body as a living sacrifice in God's service. A sacrifice requires giving up something of value to gain something of greater value. Serving God is so important we should dedicate our bodies for that purpose.

Matthew 6:19-24,33 – Lay up treasure in heaven, not on earth. You can't serve two masters, so seek *first* God's kingdom and righteousness. Pleasing God and receiving eternal life must be top priority to Christians.

Matthew 16:24-27 – True followers of Jesus must deny self, give our lives in God's service, and recognize that the soul is more valuable than the whole world.

What are your priorities? Is being right with God the most important thing in your life, or are you more interested in money, job, family, possessions, recreation, entertainment, etc.? If faithfulness to God has not been your main priority, then it must become your priority if you want eternal life.

(See also 2 Corinthians 5:14,15; Ecclesiastes 12:13; Colossians 3:1,2; 2 Corinthians 8:5; Matthew 10:34-37; Galatians 2:20.)

Obeying God Is Essential.

James 1:21-27 – Knowing God's will is not enough; to have God's blessing we must be obedient. Many people are religious, but unless they know and practice the truth, their religion is worthless.

Luke 6:46 – Confessing Jesus as Lord is also not enough. We must do what Jesus says. (Matthew 7:21-28)

1 John 2:3-6 – If we say we know God but we don't obey Him, we are liars. To know that we know Him, we must keep His commands and walk as He walked.

Have you been living obediently since you became God's child? If not, if you want Him to accept you, you must determine to obey.

(See also Romans 6:1-18; John 14:15,21-24; 1 John 5:3; 3:6-10; Matthew 28:20; Hebrews 5:9; Acts 10:34,35; Galatians 5:6; James 2:14-26.)

Continue Steadfast to the End.

Of those who begin serving God, too many fall by the wayside. Beginning is useless unless we continue till death.

Galatians 6:7-9 – To reap eternal life, we must not grow weary or get discouraged with doing good. If we let problems and hindrances stop our work for the Lord, we will reap corruption.

1 Corinthians 15:58 – Be steadfast, immovable, always abounding in the Lord's work, because labor for the Lord is not vain.

Matthew 10:22 – We must endure and be faithful to the end: to the point of death (Revelation 2:10).

What does God see when He looks at your life? Have you continued patiently doing God's will, or have you fallen into sin? If you have not been faithful, you must make up your mind to serve Him till death, whatever the future may hold.

(See also Romans 2:6-10; Luke 8:15; Hebrews 10:35,36; 6:12,15; 3:14; Colossians 1:10,11; Revelation 2:2,3; James 5:7,8; 1:12.)

But God's Children Often Become Unfaithful.

Though God says we should continue to obey, in practice we often become disobedient and deserve to be punished.

The Danger of Falling

Hebrews 3:12-14 – Because of their sins, God would not let Israel enter the promised rest (verses 7-11). Hebrew Christians faced the same danger: an evil heart of unbelief, departing from God, being hardened by the deceit of sin. We partake of Christ only if we continue steadfast to the end.

1 Corinthians 9:27; 10:1-12 – Again Israel serves as an example to us: we must take heed lest we fall and disobey God. Even Paul could be rejected if he failed to properly control himself.

Despite God's warnings, the truth is that His children sometimes become unfaithful. It even happens to elders, deacons, preachers, teachers, etc. It can happen to anyone, if we are not careful. Has it happened to you?

(See also Ezekiel 33:12,13,18; 18:20-26; 2 Peter 2:20-22; Galatians 5:1-4; Hebrews 10:26-31,39; 1 John 1:8-2:2.)

Examples of Falling Away

Adam and Eve (Genesis 3) – Adam and Eve were in God's fellowship since creation; but they sinned, leading to suffering and death. They teach us about the danger of falling (2 Corinthians 11:3).

David (2 Samuel 11 and 12) – David committed adultery with Bathsheeba, then had her husband killed to cover up. Though he repented in bitter grief, he suffered consequences for years. (Compare Psalm 51:1-11; 32:1-5.)

The prodigal son (Luke 15:11-3) – The son wasted his father's inheritance on harlots, leading to severe consequences. He finally repented and returned to the father. What about us: have we committed sins we should repent of?

Peter (Matthew 26:69-75) – Though he was an apostle, Peter denied Jesus three times, even swearing that he did not know Jesus. Afterward, he felt horrible grief. If he could sin, surely it is also possible for us. Yet he repented and eventually became one of Jesus' most effective workers. Are we willing to repent of our sins?

Simon the sorcerer (Acts 8:12-24) – Simon obeyed the gospel but later sinned by trying to buy the power of imparting the Holy Spirit. He was told that he was in iniquity and must repent or perish.

Sometimes Christians become over-confident about sin: "It can't happen to me." Or we lack a sense of guilt and godly sorrow for our sins. But if it could happen to these people, it can happen to us. And sin carries serious consequences. We need to take it seriously.

(See also 1 Corinthians 10:1-12; Numbers 20:2-13; 2 Timothy 4:10; Jeremiah 3:6-22; 14:7; example of King Saul.)

God Wants His Children to Be Saved.

We need to be concerned about sin, but sometimes people become overburdened by guilt till they think their case is hopeless and they may as well give up. Consider God's provisions for our salvation.

God Is Willing to Forgive.

All the people we just studied committed grievous sins, yet God was willing to forgive every one of them. If so, then He is also willing to forgive us.

Isaiah 55:6,7 – God offered to forgive Israel if they would repent. He has no pleasure in the death of the wicked. He wants to save, not punish. He offers mercy and abundant pardon.

1 John 1:8-2:2 – God warns us plainly not to sin, but He also states the reality that we all do sin. When we sin, Jesus is our Advocate and Propitiation. He died, not just for the world, but for God's children who sin. God is willing to forgive and cleanse us from all unrighteousness.

Luke 15:4-10,20-24 – Jesus taught three stories: the lost sheep, the lost coin, and the prodigal son. All of them teach that God wants sinners to repent, and we should want it too. The great efforts to restore what was lost, and the great joy when it was found, all show how much God really wants to save His children when they sin.

Let us appreciate the seriousness of sin. But let us also appreciate the fact that God's grace is greater than sin (Romans 5:20; 1 Timothy 1:13,14). Let us not despair because of our sins, but come back to Him in great humility, trusting in His love for us.

(Ezekiel 18:21-23; Jeremiah 3:13-22; 36:3,7; Hosea 14:4; 2 Peter 3:9; 1 Timothy 2:4,6; Titus 2:11; John 3:16; Romans 5:6-10; Luke 5:32; 19:10; Ephesians 1:7; Hebrews 7:25)

God Uses His Word and Other Christians to Restore Us.

Revelation 3:19 – Jesus reproves and chastens those whom He loves. He does this through His word that reveals our sins and urges us to repent. This bothers our conscience, but this is needed because God loves us and doesn't want to punish us. (Hebrews 12:5-12; 2 Timothy 3:16,17)

James 5:19,20 – Other Christians have a God-given duty to talk to us about our sins. If we resent this, remember that God commanded it as part of His plan for restoring us. (Galatians 6:1,2; 2 Timothy 2:24-26; 4:2; Luke 17:3,4; 1 Timothy 5:20; Ezekiel 33:1-9; Proverbs 10:17; 13:18; 15:31-33; 24:24,25; 25:12; 28:4,23; 29:1)

2 Thessalonians 3:6,14,15 – If we refuse to repent when rebuked, the church must go further and withdraw from us. This is also an act of love done in obedience to God's command for our good, to motivate us to repent. (Matthew 18:15-17; 1 Corinthians 5; Titus 3:10; Romans 16:17,18)

We Can Serve God Faithfully.

Some people become so discouraged over sin that they think serving God is so hard they cannot possibly succeed.

1 Corinthians 10:13 – Having warned us to guard against falling (verses 1-12), God assures us He will not allow any temptations beyond our ability to handle with His help. He always makes a way of escape (this does not mean the temptation will go away, but we can be faithful in spite of it).

Ephesians 6:10-18 – God provides all the weapons we need to fight Satan. God's armor supplies the strength we need to withstand every temptation. To succeed, we must be familiar with our weapons and use them diligently.

Philippians 4:13 – We can do all things through Christ who strengthens us. If we trust our own strength alone, Satan will defeat us. But there is never any reason to fail if we rely upon God's strength.

If you have been in sin, you must trust God that you can be forgiven and serve Him faithfully. Growing in Christ takes time, but you can do it. Are you willing to use God's strength so you can be faithful and receive eternal life?

(See also 1 Peter 5:6-10; 2 Timothy 3:15-17; Romans 8:31-39; 1 Peter 1:3-5; 1 John 5:3; 2 Peter 1:3; Ephesians 3:20,21; Joshua 1:5-9; 2 Corinthians 10:4,5; 9:8-10; Philippians 4:6,7.)

Erring Children Must Meet Conditions to Be Forgiven.

If a child of God needs forgiveness and wants to make his life right with God, what must he do?

Repent of Sins.

Matthew 21:28-32 – A son refused to do the work his father told him to do, but later he repented and went. So we must repent when we have disobeyed God. Repentance is a change of mind in which we decide to cease living in sin and return to doing God's will.

Acts 8:22 – When Simon sinned, Peter told him to repent and pray for forgiveness.

2 Corinthians 7:10 – Godly sorrow produces repentance to salvation. If we are truly sorry for our sins, we will determine to live obediently. Repentance is so vital to our salvation that it is the turning point. No one ceases sin until they decide to cease. Have you repented of your sins?

(See also Psalm 38:18; Revelation 2:5; 3:19; Romans 2:4,5; Ezekiel 18:30-32; 2 Timothy 2:25,26.)

Pray for Forgiveness.

Acts 8:22 – Simon was told to repent and pray for forgiveness.

1 John 1:9 – God is faithful and just to forgive us if we confess our sins. Don't be too ashamed to talk to God about your sins. He wants to forgive, but we must ask.

Proverbs 28:13 – If we cover our sins we won't prosper. We must confess and forsake them to have mercy. Don't think you can hide from God or that He will forget your sins, if you just quit doing them. We must admit guilt and ask for forgiveness. Say it!

Note that only children of God are told to pray for forgiveness when they sin. When people have never been baptized, they are told to repent of sin, confess Christ, and be baptized to receive forgiveness (Mark 16:15,16; Romans 1:16; 10:9,10,17; Acts 2:38; 17:30; Romans 6:3,4; Acts 22:16). But if you have done this and gone back into sin, then you must repent and pray.

(See also Matthew 6:12; Luke 18:13; 2 Chronicles 7:14; Psalm 51:1-14; 32:1-5; 38:18.)

Correct Any Harm Done to Others.

If your sin is known only to you and God, then all that is needed is repentance, prayer, and a corrected life. But if others have been hurt by the sin, or if others know about it, then more is required.

Apologize to people you have personally harmed.

Matthew 5:23,24 – In order for God to accept our worship, we must do what we can to right the wrongs we have done to others. Go to them and be reconciled.

James 5:16 – Confessing to others may help for any sin; but when we have personally wronged others, then it is essential to confess to them.

Luke 15:18,21 – The prodigal son had sinned, not just against heaven (God), but also against his father. He wasted his father's money in evil living. So he arose, went to the one he had wronged, and said, "I have sinned against heaven **and** in your sight."

We cannot be forgiven if we are too proud or too cowardly to admit sin and ask for forgiveness. Don't seek a minimal confession. Go to the one wronged and say, "I have sinned. I repent. Please forgive me." (Luke 17:3,4)

Make restitution (where possible).

Sometimes we commit sins that have continuing consequences: other people may continue to be hurt in ways that confession alone will not solve. We are obligated to try to eliminate those harmful effects to the extent that we can.

Ezekiel 33:14,15 – If a wicked man turns from sin and determines to do right, he must return anything he stole. This is called "restitution": compensation for loss. (Leviticus 6:1-5; Numbers 5:5-8; 2 Samuel 12:6; Exodus 22:1-15; 1 Samuel 12:3)

Matthew 21:28-31 – When the son repented, it was not enough just to decide to do right next time. In order to correct the effects of his wrong, he had to do the job that he had wrongly refused to do.

Luke 19:8 – Zacchaeus said he would restore four times whatever he had wrongly taken from others.

Unfortunately, the harm caused by some sins (such as murder) is impossible to completely undo. Nevertheless, to the extent of our ability, we must compensate others for the harm our wrongs caused.

(See also Philemon 10-14,18,19; Ezra 9:1-10:44; Nehemiah 5:1-13; Proverbs 6:30,31; Acts 16:33; 26:20; 19:18,19.)

Acknowledge our repentance to members of the church, if our sin is known.

Galatians 6:1 – If other members know about our sin, they must make sure we are reproved. It follows that we must tell them when we repent, so they will know they no longer need to rebuke us. (Luke 17:3,4; James 5:19,20; etc. – see Scriptures listed previously.)

2 Thessalonians 3:6,14,15 – If we persistently refuse to repent, the church must withdraw from us. It follows that, when we repent, we must let them know so they can accept us back as faithful members, forgive us, and comfort us. If we don't let them know when we repent, they must continue treating us as unrepentant sinners. (See 2 Corinthians 2:5-11; Luke 17:3,4; Matthew 6:12-15; 18:21-35.)

Matthew 18:6,7; Hebrews 12:15 – When other people know we have sinned, this causes a stumbling block and discouragement. We set a bad example and a harmful influence. The principle of restitution requires us to overcome this harm when possible. To do this, we must let them know we have repented. (See also 1 Timothy 4:12; Titus 2:7,8; Proverbs 28:10; Luke 17:1,2; Romans 14:21; 1 Corinthians 8:12; 5:6.)

2 Peter 2:1,2; 1 Timothy 5:14; 6:1 – If our sins are known outside the church, this also harms other members because it hinders their

efforts to save the lost. It causes the way of truth to be evil spoken of. Again, restitution would require us to let others know when we have repented.

(See also Proverbs 22:1; 2 Corinthians 8:21; Ecclesiastes 10:1; Romans 2:24; 1:18; 2 Corinthians 6:3; 8:21; Titus 2:5,8; 1 Peter 2:12; 3:16; 1 Thessalonians 4:12; 2 Samuel 12:14.)

Then Remain Faithful.

Acts 26:20; Luke 3:8,9 – We must bring forth fruits of repentance: follow through and make the changes in conduct that we have decided to make.

Matthew 21:28,29 – The son repented and then did what he had been told.

Proverbs 28:13 – Having confessed our sins, we must forsake them.

(See also Ezekiel 18:21-23,27,28,30-32; 33:11-16; Revelation 2:4,5; Isaiah 55:6,7; Jeremiah 18:11.)

Conclusion

Why should you return to God's service?

(1) Because God is your Maker and Master (Luke 6:46; Ecclesiastes 12:13).

(2) Because God loves you, and you should love God (1 John 4:19; 5:3; John 14:15).

(3) Because Jesus died to save you (2 Corinthians 5:14,15; Romans 5:6-10).

(4) So you can have eternal life instead of eternal punishment (Romans 2:5-10; Matthew 25:46).

If you are a child of God who is guilty of sin, we urge you to repent, pray for forgiveness, correct the harm done by your sin, and then live a life of faithful service to God.

How Many Ways to Salvation through Jesus?

Introduction:

John 14:6 – Jesus said, "I am the way, the truth, and the life. No one comes to the Father except through Me." So no one can be saved except through Jesus. (Acts 4:12; John 8:24)

Question: Is there more than one way to be saved by Jesus?

Could it be that Jesus saves different people in different ways? Some are baptized, but could it be that others just believe and others are saved even without believing? Some are members of a church, but could others be saved outside the church? Could it be that Jesus accepts them all?

Ultimately, these questions are raised in order to justify people in different faiths and denominations. Many sincere people are following different paths. Could it be that the different paths still lead to Jesus? "We are all going to the same place, just by different roads."

Let us consider things the Scripture says everyone one must follow to be saved.

Notice, not just *what* the gospel says to do, but also *how many* people must do them. Are some requirements of the gospel just for some people, and different requirements for others? Or are all people required to do these things? Consider the following:

Jesus' Death

John 3:16 – God so loved the **world** that He gave His only begotten Son, that **whoever** believes in Him should not perish but have everlasting life. Jesus' death is for the whole world.

1 Timothy 2:6 – He gave Himself a ransom for **all**.

Hebrews 2:9 – By the grace of God He tasted death for **everyone**.

2 Corinthians 5:15 – He died for **all**.

So, the only way to be saved is through Jesus; but the only way to be saved through Jesus is through His death. Jesus offers no other way to salvation. This is generally acknowledged by people who recognize that salvation must come through Jesus.

So the question now is: How do we receive forgiveness through His death? Is there more than one way to be saved by His death, or must all meet the same conditions?

The Gospel

Romans 1:16 – The gospel of Christ is the power of God to salvation for **everyone** who believes, for the Jew first and also for the Greek.

Mark 16:15 – Jesus said to go into **all the world** and preach the gospel to **every** creature.

Galatians 1:8,9 – **Anyone** who preaches a different gospel is accursed.

So, the gospel is the message that tells us how to be saved through Jesus' death. And there is only one true gospel. We must not change or tamper with it. It is the same for all. That gospel is completely revealed in the Scriptures (2 Timothy 3:16,17).

Since the gospel is the only way to learn about salvation through Jesus, then does the gospel allow more than one way to benefit from Jesus' death, or is there only one way?

(Revelation 22:18,19; 2 Thessalonians 2:14; Acts 20:32)

Hearing or Learning the Gospel

John 6:44,45 – Jesus said, "**No** one can come to Me unless the Father who sent Me draws him. They shall **all** be taught by God. Therefore, **everyone** who has heard and learned from the Father comes to Me." But we already learned that the gospel is the message the Father uses to teach people and draw them to Jesus. So all must **learn** the gospel in order to come to Jesus.

Mark 16:15 – Jesus said, "Go into all the **world** and preach the gospel to **every** creature."

Romans 10:17 – So then faith comes by hearing, and hearing by the word of God.

So, the gospel is the power of God to salvation (Romans 1:16), because it tells people how to be saved by the death of Jesus. And since there is only one gospel, no one has the right to preach a different gospel. The gospel we must learn is the same for all.

But what does the gospel say? Does it allow people to be saved in various ways?

(Matt. 11:28,29; Acts 3:22,23)

Faith

Romans 1:16 – The gospel is the power of God to salvation for **everyone** who **believes**.

John 3:16 – God so loved the **world** that He gave His only begotten Son, that **whoever believes** in Him should not perish but have everlasting life.

Mark 16:15,16 – The gospel preached to the **whole world** says that **whoever believes** and is baptized will be saved. But those who do not **believe** will be condemned.

John 8:24 – Jesus said, "If you do not **believe** that I am He, you will die in your sins."

Ephesians 4:4-6 – There is one body and one Spirit, just as you were called in one hope of your calling; one Lord, **one faith**, one baptism; one God and Father of all, who is above all, and through all, and in you all.

So faith is a universal condition to salvation through Jesus' death. All must believe the gospel of Jesus. Those who do not believe will die in sin. Do you believe?

Many people would agree that we must have faith, but salvation requires believing there is "**one** faith." Not only must we learn the gospel, we must all learn the **same** gospel. Not only must all believe, we must all have the **same** faith. We begin to see that the way to salvation is narrow.

Repentance

Repentance is a change of mind in which we recognize we have been wrong and we decide to change and do right. Note what the gospel of Jesus says about it.

Acts 17:30 – God commands **all men everywhere** to repent.

2 Peter 3:9 – The Lord is not willing that **any** should perish but that **all** should come to repentance. So all must repent or perish.

Acts 2:38,39 – Repent, and let **every one of you** be baptized in the name of Jesus Christ for the remission of sins. This promise is to **all who are afar off, as many as the Lord our God will call**.

The gospel teaches that all men everywhere must repent or perish. So, repentance is another universal requirement for salvation.

Have you repented of your sins and determined to live your life for God?

(Luke 13:3,5; 24:47)

Obedience

Many will accept all that we have learned to this point, yet many believe people can be saved without doing anything. They say obedience is not essential. What does the gospel say?

Hebrews 5:9 – Jesus became the author of eternal salvation to **all** who **obey** Him.

Matthew 7:24-27 – **Whoever** hears Jesus' sayings and **does** them has a house that will not fall. **Everyone** who does not **do** them has a house that will fall. (Compare verses 21-23.)

Romans 2:6-11 – The Lord will judge **each** one according to his **deeds** (verse 6). Eternal life is for those who **do** good (verse 7), **everyone** who **works** what is good, Jew or Greek (verse 10). But indignation and wrath are for those who do not **obey** the truth (verse 8); this is true of **every soul of man** who does evil, Jew or Greek (verse 9). (2 Corinthians 5:10)

Acts 10:34,35 – God shows no partiality. But in **every** nation **whoever** fears Him and **works** righteousness is accepted by Him.

2 Thessalonians 1:8,9 – Jesus will come in flaming fire taking vengeance on those who do not know God, and on those who do not **obey the gospel of our Lord Jesus Christ**.

Contrary to what some think, no one can be saved without obedience. It is not true that some who obey will be saved but others will be saved without obedience.

So here is another universal requirement of the gospel. To be saved, all must be obedient. The one gospel that we must all learn and the one faith that we must all believe say that obedience is necessary in order for us to be forgiven of our sins by the blood of Jesus.

The path becomes more and more narrow. What does this obedience include?

(Matthew 12:50; John 14:23; James 1:23-25; Romans 1:5)

Confession of Christ

Matthew 10:32,33 – **Whoever** confesses Me before men, him I will also confess before My Father in heaven. But whoever denies Me before men, him I will also deny before My Father.

1 John 4:15 – **Whoever** confesses that Jesus is God's Son, God abides in him, and he in God.

Romans 10:9,10 – If you confess with your mouth the Lord Jesus and believe in your heart that God has raised Him from the dead, you will be saved. For with the heart one believes unto righteousness, and with the mouth confession is made unto salvation.

So confession is another universal requirement of salvation: everyone must confess Christ to be saved. Many people would agree that this is true. But notice that this is an outward act of obedience. If confession is required, then outward acts are required to be saved. To deny the need for outward acts would be to deny the need for confession.

The gospel, that all must learn and all must believe, says that confession is another universal requirement of salvation. Have you confessed Christ as your Lord and Savior?

Baptism

Baptism is another condition of obedience according to the gospel. Yet some think that people can be saved whether or not they have been baptized. Is baptism another universal requirement of salvation by faith in Christ according to the gospel?

Mark 16:15,16 – Go into **all the world** and preach the gospel to **every creature**. He who believes and is **baptized** will be saved. The one gospel, that everyone must hear, believe, and obey, requires every creature in all the world to be baptized to be saved.

John 3:3,5 – Unless one is born again of **water** and the Spirit, he cannot enter the kingdom of God. So no one can enter the kingdom unless he is born again of water. But the only New Testament practice that requires water is baptism.

Acts 2:38,39 – Repent, and let ***every one of you*** be ***baptized*** in the name of Jesus Christ for the remission of sins. This promise is to ***all who are afar off, as many as the Lord our God will call***.

So people who need remission of sins must not only repent, they must also be baptized. This is required of "every one" and "all who are afar, as many as the Lord will call." But this call is extended through the gospel (2 Thessalonians 2:14), which should be preached to whole world.

Romans 6:3,4 – ***As many*** of us as were ***baptized*** into Christ Jesus were ***baptized*** into His death … Therefore we were buried with Him through ***baptism*** into death, so we should walk in newness of life. (Note that baptism is a burial, i.e., an immersion.)

So we have learned that everyone must be saved by the death of Jesus, but how many people have contacted that death? As many as have been baptized. When we have been baptized, then we walk in newness of life (we are born again, which confirms what we learned in John 3:3,5). (Compare 2 Corinthians 5:17.)

Galatians 3:26,27 – For you are ***all*** sons of God through faith in Christ Jesus. For ***as many of you as*** were ***baptized*** into Christ have put on Christ. So, we must all believe the one faith, and we are all children of God (born again) through faith. But we come into Christ by faith when we are baptized. The number of those in Christ is the same as the number of those baptized. So, all must be baptized to be in Christ.

Contrary to common thinking, baptism is a universal requirement for salvation, just like hearing, believing, repentance, and confession. The one gospel, that all must hear and believe, requires that all be baptized to receive remission of sins, contact Jesus' death, come into Jesus, and be saved. Have you been baptized to receive the remission of your sins?

(Matthew 28:18,19)

Church Membership

Since baptism puts one into the church, the same people who deny that baptism is necessary will also generally deny that church membership is necessary to salvation. By this, however, they usually mean membership in a denomination. But what does the one gospel, that we must all believe to be saved, say about church membership?

All the saved are in Jesus' church.

Matthew 16:18 – Jesus planned and built His church. Note that it is one church, not many different churches. Jesus has a church, but it is not a denomination.

Acts 2:47 – The Lord adds to His church daily those who are being **saved**. So, **all** people need to be saved; but when the are saved, they are added to the church that Jesus began. To be saved is to become part of the church. So how can one be saved outside the church?

Acts 20:28 – Jesus purchased the **church** with His own blood. But **everyone** must be cleansed by Jesus' blood to be saved. Since the people that He purchased with His blood make up the church, how can anyone be saved outside the church?

Ephesians 5:23,25 – For the husband is head of the wife, as Christ is head of the church, and He is the Savior of the **body**. Christ also loved the **church** and gave Himself for her. The church is the body over which Christ is the Head (compare 1:22,23).

The church does not save us; Jesus saves us. But He is the Savior of the body. He gave Himself for the church. So those whom He saves are **all** in the body, the church.

The church that belongs to Jesus is one united body.

Since the Head has only one body, and since a man may be husband to only one wife, it likewise follows that there is only one true church. The church that Jesus built is not a denomination.

Ephesians 4:3-6 – Keeping the unity of the Spirit in the bond of peace requires us to accept just one true God and Father, one true hope, one true faith, one true baptism, etc. In the same way, there is one true body, which is the church.

Scriptural unity requires that **all** the saved are included in "one body," the church. This one body believes and teaches the "one faith." We must not approve the existence of different bodies with different faiths, any more than we approve of different Gods. (2:14,16; Colossians 3:15)

1 Corinthians 12:20 – There are many members, yet **one body**. As individuals are saved, they become members of the body, but there is only one true body. Those who are saved have all been baptized into one body (verse 13), so **all** are members of that one body, the church (verse 12).

Jesus' church is not a denomination, nor does it consist of different denominations. It is the body that consists of **all** saved people. That one body must teach and believe the one faith, with no human changes. This includes teaching the truth about salvation. And it must work to maintain unity, not justifying or accepting division (1 Corinthians 1:10-13; 12:25; John 17:20-23; Galatians 5:19-21; Luke 11:17; Romans 16:17).

So the one gospel, that all must learn and believe without changing, requires that all saved people be part of one church. Membership in Jesus' church is therefore another universal requirement of salvation. Are you a member of Jesus' one true church? (Romans 12:4,5)

Faithful Living

When a person is baptized, all his past sins are forgiven and he comes into Christ. The Lord then adds him to His one church, the body of all saved people. It is possible afterward, however, for disciples to go astray into error. What are the consequences?

Matthew 28:19,20 – Having been baptized, disciples from **all nations** should be taught to **observe** all things that Jesus has commanded. Baptism simply begins a life of obedience.

John 15:6 – If **anyone** does not abide in Jesus, he is cast out as a branch and is withered; and they gather them and throw them into the fire, and they are burned. (Compare verse 2.)

2 Corinthians 5:15 – Christ died for **all**, that people should live no longer for themselves, but for Him who died for them and rose again. **Everyone** must be saved by Jesus' death, but that means we must **all** live for Him.

Hebrews 3:12-14 – **Any** one can depart from God through the deceitfulness of sin. We partake of Christ only if we hold our confidence steadfast to the end. (4:11)

2 John 9 – **Whoever** transgresses and does not abide in the doctrine of Christ does not have God. He who abides in the doctrine of Christ has both the Father and the Son.

So after baptism, all are required to continue to live faithfully in order to maintain their relationship with the Lord. This includes repenting and confessing sins we may commit. Continuing to live faithfully after conversion is another universal requirement to ultimately receive eternal life through Jesus. Are you living faithfully in the Lord's service?

(Hebrews 12:15; 10:38; Matthew 16:24-27; James 5:19,20; 2 John 9-11)

Conclusion

By studying the individual requirements of salvation, we have learned that **all** people must obey **all** of these conditions in order to be saved. It follows that there is only one way to salvation through Jesus for all people. Other gospel passages confirm this conclusion:

Romans 2:6-11 – God does not show **partiality** (verse 11). **Everyone** who works good receives eternal life, but **every** soul who does evil receives tribulation and anguish. This confirms that the conditions of salvation are the same for all; otherwise, God would be showing partiality. (Acts 10:34,35)

Matthew 7:13,14 – There is just one gate and one way leading to life. It is narrow and difficult. Few find it. Most are on the broad road to destruction.

Remember that no one has a right to teach a different gospel (Galatians 1:8,9). It follows that these conditions apply to all people, and no one has the right to teach a different gospel.

Have you obeyed these conditions of forgiveness? Have you received forgiveness by the death of Jesus? Are you living a faithful life as a member of Jesus' one true church?

Printed books, booklets, and tracts available at
www.lighttomypath.net/sales
Free Bible study articles online at
www.gospelway.com
Free Bible courses online at www.biblestudylessons.com
Free class books at www.biblestudylessons.com/classbooks
Free commentaries on Bible books at
www.gospelway.com/commentary
Contact the author at
www.gospelway.com/comments
Free e-mail Bible study newsletter –
www.gospelway.com/update_subscribe.htm

Made in the USA
Las Vegas, NV
15 November 2020